THE CHARACTER OF THE DEACON

The Character of the Deacon

SPIRITUAL AND PASTORAL FOUNDATIONS

EDITED BY James Keating

Paulist Press
New York / Mahwah, NJ

Unless otherwise stated, the Scripture quotations contained herein are from the *New American Bible, Revised Edition* © 2010, 1991, 1986, 1970 Confraternity of Christian Doctrine, Washington, D.C. and are used by permission of the copyright owner. All Rights Reserved. No part of the New American Bible may be reproduced in any form without permission in writing from the copyright owner.

Cover image photo of the fresco *The Sermon of St. Stephen* by Fra Angelico courtesy of Wikimedia Commons (Web Gallery of Art)
Cover and book design by Lynn Else

Copyright © 2017 by James Keating

All rights reserved. No part of this publication may be reproduced, stored in a retrieval system, or transmitted in any form or by any means, electronic, mechanical, photocopying, recording, scanning, or otherwise, without either the prior written permission of the Publisher, or authorization through payment of the appropriate per-copy fee to the Copyright Clearance Center, Inc., 222 Rosewood Drive, Danvers, MA 01923, (978) 750-8400, fax (978) 646-8600, or on the Web at www.copyright.com. Requests to the Publisher for permission should be addressed to the Permissions Department, Paulist Press, 997 Macarthur Boulevard, Mahwah, NJ 07430, (201) 825-7300, fax (201) 825-8345, or online at www.paulistpress.com.

Library of Congress Cataloging-in-Publication Data:
Names: Keating, James, editor.
Title: The character of the deacon : spiritual and pastoral foundations / edited by James Keating.
Description: New York : Paulist Press, 2017. | Includes bibliographical references and index.
Identifiers: LCCN 2016018010 (print) | LCCN 2016028831 (ebook) | ISBN 9780809153060 (pbk. : alk. paper) | ISBN 9781587686436 (ebook)
Subjects: LCSH: Deacons.
Classification: LCC BX1912 .C48 2017 (print) | LCC BX1912 (ebook) | DDC 262/.142–dc23
LC record available at https://lccn.loc.gov/2016018010

ISBN 978-0-8091-5306-0 (paperback)
ISBN 978-1-58768-643-6 (e-book)

Published by Paulist Press
997 Macarthur Boulevard
Mahwah, New Jersey 07430

www.paulistpress.com

Printed and bound in the
United States of America

In memory of Deacon Alan LeClair (1948–2015),
of the Archdiocese of Omaha, and to
his beloved wife, Mitzi

Contents

Foreword by Bishop Michael F. Burbidge ix

Introduction xi

Part I: Diaconate and Scripture **1**

1. From Being with Jesus to Proclaiming the Word –
   Scott M. Carl 3

2. The Mystery of Jesus as Deacon – *Stephen F. Miletic* 24

3. Christ as Servant – *William M. Wright* 44

Part II: Diaconate and Tradition **59**

4. The Uniqueness of the Deacon – *W. Shawn McKnight* . . . 61

5. Rahner in Retrospect – *Frederick Christian Bauerschmidt* 85

Part III: Diaconate and Prayer **101**

6. The *Lex Orandi* of the Ordination Rite –
   David W. Fagerberg 103

7. Identity and Holiness – *James Keating* 122

Part IV: Diaconate and Action **139**

8. Identity and Mission – *Dominic Cerrato* 141

About the Contributors 169

Foreword

The generous service of deacons has been a special blessing to me and to all of the faithful in this local church of the diocese of Raleigh, where I serve as the bishop. Made possible by the restoration of the Permanent Diaconate at the Second Vatican Council, their presence has provided a powerful sign, in both the workplace and in the home, of the gospel permeating society, and embodies the injunction of St. Polycarp to deacons in the third century: "Let them be merciful and zealous, and let them walk according to the truth of the Lord, who became the servant of all" (LG 29).

The Character of the Deacon is an excellent resource for those in formation for this beautiful vocation—whether it be the transitional or permanent diaconate. It is also useful for those who have a general interest in the study of its history and theological development. Significantly, through the history and development of the diaconate, it explains in detail that such vocations were not a result of a dearth in priestly vocations, but rather are always found in concert with the pastoral and spiritual ministry of the priesthood in the life of the Church. Consequently, to understand the diaconate is to reflect more completely on the sacrament of holy orders in its totality.

As we engage in this reflection, it becomes clear that the diaconate, today, is of significance within the ongoing work of evangelization. Our preference to serve those who are ill, in prison, and most in need—highlighted so powerfully in the pontificate of Pope Francis—is reflected in the diaconate. Furthermore, the deacons can proclaim the gospel, especially to those who may be drawn to the inherent good of assisting others, yet may have never encountered our Lord as the very foundation of these gestures of human compassion and love.

The Character of the Deacon

In reflecting more deeply on the diaconate and its communion with all clergy, those in consecrated life and the laity, it is my hope that, through this resource, our Lord will bless you anew with the joy of the gospel and an increased ardor for the Catholic faith. May he guide you always in the vocation to which he has called you and in your service to his Church and her mission, especially toward those yet to hear his voice.

Most Reverend Michael F. Burbidge
Bishop of Raleigh
Chair, USCCB Committee on Clergy,
Consecrated Life and Vocations

Introduction

The deacon's primary ministry is twofold: to serve at the altar and ambo and from such service be sent by Christ, while always abiding with him in prayer, to respond to the spiritual and corporeal needs of people.[1]

As one who serves at the altar, the deacon is called to contemplate him whose blood he consumes and distributes. This contemplation leads him to pray that Christ's own charity will fill his conscience, and in turn, the mystery of this charity fires his presence at the altar of daily work, commitment, and sacrifice. The deacon holds the blood, consumes the blood, and then publicly confesses that he lives by the blood that is given to him in the Spirit—the Spirit who broods over the sacrifice of the Eucharist.

The deacon must approach the mystery of the blood of Christ with a unique supplication. "Lord, how might I minister your life-blood in the Church and as a healing agent in the culture?" Out of diaconal obedience (i.e., entrusted with a mission) to the bishop and diaconal love for the mystery of the Eucharist and Word flow the ordinary and often hidden presence of the deacon incarnating an ordained ministerial presence in the fabric of culture.

It is good to let the blood of Christ enter us in silence so as to bring us to interior change, a change of heart, a transformation that will give birth to peace, a peace out of which will flow all future ministry.

The purpose of diaconal formation is to create an opportunity for a man to be moved by God into a new life. This new life is characterized by the deep belief that God takes care of the candidate's own needs so that he is now free to respond to the needs of others. This is the blood that flows through the deacon, the blood of a new life of freedom, a Divine freedom received according to the man's capacity to trust in faith. To submit to formation is to submit to the power of the Spirit, who effects a new interiority, a conscience born of the blood of Christ, born of cooperation with grace.

The deacon wants God to continue purifying him of sinful affections and releasing him to love that is good and true and holy. In this deepest of desires, to be a holy deacon, the candidate glimpses the true end of his vocation: to be a man who shares in the life of God for the healing and benefit of the Church and culture. With a burning desire for holiness, the candidate is now ready to be ordained because he has died and his life is now "hidden with Christ in God" (Col 3:3).

The goal of this book is to bring a man in formation deeper into the sacred origins of his call from Christ. It is a vocation that seeks to affect the formation of conscience, one that wishes to secure the charity of Christ as the lodestar of conscience. At ordination, a man comes forward to the bishop and, in a vulnerability secured by formation, opens his conscience to be seared with grace. This grace impinges upon his whole being and establishes within him a new communion with the servant mysteries of Christ; a communion that is permanent, personal, and powerful. Such is the sacramental character of holy orders.

It is the hope of each of the authors that this book will not only serve as a dynamic resource for the intellectual and spiritual formation of deacons, but that it will also secure for the deacon who has ministered for many years what he only glimpsed at the beginning of his ministry—Christ called him into a vocation that is fuller and richer than he could have ever believed. *Amen!*

NOTES

1. For deeper explication on the themes present here, see James Keating, "Themes for a Canonical Retreat: The Spiritual Apex of Diaconal Formation," in William Ditewig, *Forming Deacons: Ministers of Soul and Leaven* (Mahwah, NJ: Paulist Press, 2010).

PART I
Diaconate and Scripture

1.

From Being with Jesus to Proclaiming the Word

SCOTT M. CARL

The life of the early Church demonstrates the development of the office of deacon. As J. Galot, SJ, says:

> In the New Testament writings, the terms bishop, presbyter, and deacon do not yet carry the precise meaning they will have later. Presbyter and bishop can be more or less equivalent terms. Note how the presbyters of Ephesus are called bishops in Acts 20:28. The term deacon can be applied to ministries of different ranks. Paul calls himself by this term (2 Cor 3:6; 11:23; Eph 3:7), but he uses the same term to designate other ministers inferior to the apostles in rank.[1]

He also states,

> A differentiation will set in only when the ranks of the hierarchical ministry are fixed, as is the case in the letters of Ignatius of Antioch. These letters are the first available witness to a monarchic episcopate. They

present a ministerial structure which includes the bishop, a council of presbyters, and deacons in a subordinate role. Henceforth, as this structure spreads in the Church, the terms bishop, presbyter, and deacon take on the differentiated meaning which will perdure until the present. Especially, the distinction between the role of the bishop and that of the presbyter is clearly established.[2]

As we discern the office of deacon in the ministerial structure of the Church, it is reasonable to think that the use of the title *deacon* came from how the early Church understood the word group *diakon-*; that is, the role of deacon was influenced by the use of its source words in the New Testament.[3] J. N. Collins's work is invaluable in helping us gain insight into this matter. While the New Testament does not offer clarity into this initial process through which the differentiation of the offices developed, there is, nonetheless, insight to be gained into the background of the office of deacon.[4]

Thus, there is not a specific proof-text in Scripture for the establishment of the office of deacon as we understand it today but its distinct role developed in the life of the early Church— and is being discerned anew in the current day. What can Scripture, in particular the Gospels and Acts, teach us about the background to the office of deacon?

There is evidence in Scripture that Jesus sought to establish a particular group, the Twelve, as "something that goes beyond mere function."[5] As Galot argues, Jesus "made Twelve" (Mark 3:14) and "intended to 'send them out,' as Mark says, that is, to make them his own envoys, his apostles."[6] It is important to note that the Twelve must "be with" Jesus before they are sent (Mark 3:14). This order, Galot argues, is important:

> Since the creation of the new Israel is involved, the phrase "to be with him" seems to recall the expression traditionally used to refer to the covenant. "I shall be with you," Yahweh declares to Moses, disclosing his name, "I Am who I Am," as a guarantee of his fidelity (Ex 3:12–14). Jesus was later to repeat this

promise: "...I am with you always" (Matt 28:20). This promise calls for a counterpart—a mutual relationship. The fact that Jesus is with them requires of them that they be with him.[7]

Their role includes extending concretely the covenant Christ establishes for the sake of all humans; in this role, we see the beginnings of their mediating position through which "the Christian community will achieve union with Christ." Thus, this mediating role is given to those who first "have been called to be with him."[8]

Given that there is not a precise establishment of the threefold office of holy orders in the New Testament, a study of the use of *diakon-* in the Gospels of Mark and Luke as well as the Acts of the Apostles, nonetheless, yields meaningful insight into not only the *diakonia* of Jesus but what he expected for the *diakonia* of the Twelve and those with whom they share their apostolic ministry. Finally, a brief application of these insights will be offered for those who live out their vocational call in the Church in the office whose name comes from the word group itself, the diaconate.

The significant and convincing work of J. N. Collins concerning the meaning of *diakon-* in the classical Greek period and in the New Testament itself has too often been overlooked.[9] Thus, it is important, first, to summarize key aspects of his work.

Collins bases his study of *diakon-* in the New Testament on its use and meaning in non-Christian sources over many centuries before and contemporaneous with the New Testament. He demonstrates that the meaning conveyed often connotes "something special, even dignified, about the circumstance" that if unbiblical, it has "wide religious connotations." "The root idea expressed by the words is that of the *go-between*" and commonly signifies that an action is not just done for someone but it is "*done in the name of another*," including "actions done in the service of God." "In accepting such undertakings or in having them imposed on him, the agent has a mandate as well as a personal obligation, and, if he is thus deprived of the exercise of his own authority and initiative, he has whatever 'rights and powers' the mandate extends to."[10]

In providing the necessary background, Collins then demonstrates how this classical meaning of *diakon-* is not only consistent with its use in the New Testament but how to understand its use therein. We see this congruence in the use of *diakon-* in St. Paul. "Parallels between Paul's usage and other Greek usage are linguistic in character and not mythological or even theological." By reference to classical works, we can see "what Paul was saying about his role as a medium in the communication of heavenly mysteries but is not telling us what kind of medium or διάκονος (*diakonos*) he was….He saw himself…as a man passing on heaven's word." Thus, "one would conclude that here lies the root meaning of Paul's weakness. With no power ἀρετή (*aretē*) of his own to boast of, he stands at the opposite pole to 'divine men.'"[11] In his weakness, Paul relates a message that is not his own; he acts as go-between in the name of the Lord.

In the encomium at the beginning of the Letter to the Colossians, Paul speaks with conviction about being "constituted a *diakonos* of the gospel, that is, a bearer of the message from an invisible world who stands in a singular relationship to the God who originates it."[12] In the case of Paul, we see the special nature of the Greek term *diakonos* as one who "has been appointed to the task either by heaven or by an authoritative source on earth."[13] Such an understanding of *diakon-* is consistent with what we will see in the Gospels and Acts.

DIAKON- IN THE GOSPEL OF MARK

Given the consistency of the parallel passages involving *diakon-* in the Gospels of Matthew and Mark, only the latter will be presented here. Moreover, due to space considerations, we will focus on Mark 10:42–45. However, it should be noted that Mark's four uses of *diakon-* always appear in the context of the Twelve. Mark 9:35 says so explicitly, while in Mark 10:42–45, the context is the conflict of the ten being upset at the two who were seeking special place in the Kingdom. Our main point of reference is Mark 10:45, "For the Son of Man did not come to be served (*diakonēthēnai*) but to serve (*diakonēsai*) and to give his life as a ransom for many."[14]

We note that, in both instances, *diakoneō* is used in reference to Jesus. The passive use is followed by the active. Here, Collins offers meaningful insight, "The infinitive itself, no less than the title the 'Son of man' and the prophetic verb 'came,' speaks of a particular personal commission under God, and from this point of view, the statement is at once more theological than ethical." Furthermore, adding to this perspective on these two occurrences of *diakoneō*, he says, "Because the infinitive does not indicate what the commission entails, verse 45a could hardly have existed independently, and needs to be complemented by verse 45b, which then defines the sacred role as one of ransom for many through the death of the office bearer."[15]

Collins continues, "The situation envisaged by the statement is that the Son of man is not one who holds such a position in the world as to have attendants—the διάκονοι (*diakonoi*) of the rich and powerful—coming up to him and being dispatched by him about various tasks of his own choosing; he has his own task to go to, and it is for the purpose of setting the profane grandeur of one way of life against the prophetic dedication of the other that Mark has brought these oddly fitting infinitives together."[16]

One needs the context of the entire Gospel of Mark to understand Jesus' mission as referred to in 10:45b.[17] The entire Gospel of Mark, Collins argues, answers the question about whom the Son of Man serves. This theme comes to a completion just after Jesus' death, "When the centurion who stood facing him saw how he breathed his last he said, 'Truly this man was the Son of God!'" (Mark 15:39).[18] It is the proclamation of faith in the light of Jesus' death that speaks to the power of the "ransom" he renders. Compare the voice at the baptism: "You are my beloved Son; with you I am well pleased" (Mark 1:11). Implicit here is that the *diakonia* of the Son of Man comes at God's behest. Consonant with the classical view of the word group, the *diakonia* of Jesus is his being the go-between of God and the disciples. The "message he delivers" is giving his life as a ransom for many.

The *diakonia* of Jesus, as dramatically contextualized by Mark in chapter 10, at the end of the Galilean mission and on the road to Jerusalem, was to serve the One whose voice called to him at his baptism, and the Son of Man would perform this service by carrying out the mission to which that voice had consecrated him."[19]

Jesus, too, is the "bearer of the message from an invisible world who stands in a singular relationship to the God who originates it" and it is his weakness intrinsic to the means of his ransom that shows the power of the one who originates the message.

The disciples are to follow the way of Jesus. "The Gospel that Mark proceeds to write (following the proclamation at the baptism) follows the Son's path from one proclamation of his identity to another because that was the path of the Son's calling. It was also the path that the disciples and the Markan community were called to follow."[20] What Jesus expresses in Mark 10:45 and carries out on the Cross is also to be the way of the disciples. As Moloney states,

> [Jesus'] service will take the form of his self-giving unto death, so that others might have life (v. 45b). The disciple of Jesus, called to self-giving for the sake of Jesus and the Gospel and to the service of even the most lowly, is called to *follow* Jesus. His life story, insists Mark, is the paradigm for all subsequent discipleship. The glory sought by the sons of Zebedee and the other ten (see vv. 37, 41) can be gained only through cross and service. Those who are not ashamed to take up the cross and to serve will save their lives and share in the glory of Jesus when he comes with his Father and the holy angels (see 8:38).[21]

The *diakonia* of Jesus in the Gospel of Mark is the ransom he offers through the total gift of himself on the cross; his ransom is the "message" he conveys as go-between in the name of his Father. Likewise, the *diakonia* of his disciples is to take the same shape; they perpetuate Jesus' ransom in their words and deeds in being go-betweens in his name. This will become clear later in the explanation of *diakon-* in the Gospel of Luke. As the sense of office develops in the early Church, this understanding of *diakon-* surely informs the identity of those in apostolic office in general and the diaconate in particular.

DIAKON- IN THE ACTS OF THE APOSTLES

The classical Greek use of *diakon-*, that is, as one given a task by heaven or an authoritative earthly source and so a go-between acting in the name of another, is used by Luke in the Acts of the Apostles. Regarding its use in Luke's second volume, Collins notes, "The word *diakonia* marks the major stages of Luke's history of the Christian mission. In his narrative, the term *diakonia* marks the beginning of the Twelve's mission (1:17, 25); it is there at the peak of their mission to Jerusalem (6:4); it is there to mark Paul's inclusion in the mission (20:24); and it is there when Paul completes his role in the mission (21:19)" in making his report in the presence of James and all the elders in Jerusalem.[22]

In Acts 1:8, the risen Jesus gives the commission to the Twelve to be his "witnesses in Jerusalem and in all Judea and Samaria and to the end of the earth."[23] We see this sacred commission of the Twelve with the use of *diakonia* at the beginning of their mission in Acts 1 when they are filling the hole left by Judas. As Collins notes, *diakonia* is used in the context of the Twelve up until that point when they begin sharing their ministry formally with others through prayer and the laying on of hands (Acts 6:5). Collins also provides insight into what was involved in the "*diakonein* at table" of the seven (cf. Act 6:2). Concerning Acts 6:1, Collins says that ancient readers would understand the Greek-speaking widows' missing out on their "daily *diakonia*" as "the daily preaching of the word."[24] This interpretation is aided by the immediate context of this passage in Acts. Chapter 5 ends with the apostles teaching and proclaiming the good news in the temple and at home/from house to house (*kat' oikon*); doing so in their own language (Aramaic) would leave the Greek-speaking widows in need.[25]

Thus, in Acts 6:2, the Greek-speaking widows needed someone to teach them in Greek when they gathered together around their tables.[26] The "*diakonein* at table" of Acts 6:2 would be offered by these newly appointed seven who have received the task from an authoritative source, the Twelve (Acts 6:3, 6). In Acts 6:4, the apostles "rededicate themselves to their original commission of 'ministry/*diakonia* of the word.'"[27] The passage ends with a telltale phrase of Luke in "the word of God continued to spread" (Acts 6:7), extending further the context of the passage.[28]

To sum up this passage in Acts 6, what is lacking is the daily *diakonia* for the Greek-speaking widows (Acts 6:1). The apostles do not want to neglect the Word of God to *diakonein* at table (Acts 6:2). The daily *diakonia* to the Greek-speaking widows must involve *diakonein* at table. The apostles want to appoint seven men to this task (Acts 6:3), that is, to fill in the lack of the daily *diakonia*, or in other words, to *diakonein* at table. Thus, the apostles can rededicate[29] themselves to prayer and the *diakonia* of the Word (Acts 6:4) while the seven, having been chosen and having had the apostles' hands laid upon them (Acts 6:5-6), are to fill in the lack of the "daily *diakonia*." Finally, we hear that "the word of God continued to spread" (Acts 6:7). We can conclude from these verses in Acts 6 that there is a distinction being made between what the Twelve do and what the seven have been appointed to do, yet there is also overlap, beginning with the fact that both are carrying out *diakonia*. Moreover, the overlap in activity is also seen in what we see the seven actually do as Luke's second volume continues.

Collins points out that the seven do not address people's need for food[30] but rather preach. We see this explicitly for Stephen (Acts 7:2-53); we see it for Philip, the only other member of the seven referred to thereafter, who continues the mission in Samaria (Acts 8:5), the next place Jesus told them to be witnesses following Judea (Acts 1:8). Moreover, Philip is simply referred to later as "the evangelist, who was one of the Seven" (Acts 21:8).[31] Their *diakonia* resembles the *diakonia* of the Twelve in that it involves preaching the Word.

This overlap between the apostles and the seven is further strengthened by the context of Luke's writing. As noted earlier, the immediate context for Acts 6:1-7 mentions the apostles "proclaiming (*euaggelizomenoi*) the Messiah, Jesus" (Acts 5:42). The verb *euaggelizō* is characteristic of Luke.[32] In the Gospel of Luke, the angel Gabriel *proclaims* to Mary (Luke 1:19), the angels *proclaim* to the shepherds (Luke 2:10), and John the Baptist *proclaims* (Luke 3:18), but once Jesus announces to those in Nazareth that he is *"to bring glad tidings (euaggelisasthai) to the poor"* (Luke 4:18), it is used either by Jesus (Luke 4:43; 7:22; 8:1; 16:16; 20:1) or in reference to the Twelve whom Jesus sends out to *proclaim* (Luke 9:6). In the Acts of the Apostles, the first use is in Acts 5:42, mentioned earlier, in reference to the apostles. Then four of the next five uses are in reference to Philip, one of the seven (Acts 8:4, 12; 8:35, 40; Acts 8:25 is in reference to the apostles, Peter and John). We see that the *proclaiming* that Jesus specifically does involves sending the apostles to do likewise, and this same *proclaiming* the apostles specifically do involves one of the seven doing it. Not only does the little we know about the *diakonia* of the seven resemble the *diakonia* of the Twelve, it also encompasses this technical word for *proclaiming* the Word that occupies the apostles both prior to their formal commissioning of others in Acts 6 and afterward through especially the apostolic figure of Paul. Again, we see that among the seven, whom the Twelve appointed with a *diakon*-type task, there is done the same sort of *proclaiming*.

It is, therefore, reasonable to see that the commission of the seven involved proclaiming God's Word even if we do not understand how it differs from the "prayer and *diakonia* of the word," which the Twelve so deeply desire to continue (Acts 6:4). They, too, are bearers of a message that is of another realm, go-betweens who act in the name of another.

Galot argues that the "*diakonein* at table" (Acts 6:2), which is the need the Twelve fill in light of the widows lacking in the "daily distribution" (*en tē diakonia tē kathēmerinē*) (Acts 6:1), needs to be interpreted in light of Acts 2:46: "Every day (*kath' hēmeran*) they devoted themselves to meeting together in the temple area and to breaking bread in their homes." Consequently, the "daily distribution," here, relates to the breaking of the bread done "every day" in their homes. In this manner, Galot relates the *"diakonein* at table" to the Eucharist.[33] Thus, he argues that there are eucharistic aspects for which the seven are instituted. He says that at this time the "institution was new and had no name."[34] While Galot asserts that the seven imply presbyters, given that there is not precision to the ecclesiastical offices at this point in the Church and that there is no specific designation of the seven given in Acts—which Galot admits,[35] it is best to state a more simple conclusion regarding the activity of the seven; it is possible to argue for a connection to both the proclamation of the Word and the Eucharist.

Regarding Luke's intentional use of *diakonia*, Collins notes that in Acts 20:24, Paul expresses a deep desire to complete "the διακονιαν (*diakonian*) which he received from the Lord to testify to the gospel. There are several indications here that we are dealing with a sacred commission to preach…the task involves testifying to the gospel, it is imposed by the Lord, and both the circumstances of the address and the association with the course he is running connote an itinerant mission." Another aspect of the word's meaning in the classical world is seen by its next use in Acts that relates Paul speaking to those in Jerusalem '"the things God had done among the Gentiles through his διακονιας (*diakonias*) (Acts 21:19).' The concluding phrase reads most naturally as 'through his agency….'"[36]

In conclusion, and as Collins states, "Luke has worked the code word (*diakonia*) across his long narrative to indicate how he understands the complementary nature of the roles of the major evangelizers, the Twelve and Paul."[37] Luke's use of *euaggelizō* also strengthens this assertion. After the uses mentioned above in reference to Philip, seven of the last nine uses of *euaggelizō* in Acts are used either by or in reference to Paul (with Barnabas: Acts 14:7, 15, 21; 15:35; included in the "we" of 16:10) or just to Paul alone (Acts 13:32; 17:18).[38] A key aspect to those who share in the *diakonia* of the apostles is their role in proclaiming (*euaggelizō*) the good news about Jesus.

Therefore, Luke's use of *diakonia* in Acts began with reference to the Twelve and gets extended in an intentional way to the broadened sense of "apostle" that develops as the second volume progresses. An important part of this development is in Acts 6:1-7, which confers on others at least a share in the *diakonia* of the Twelve. Thus, we can see how instructive the concept of *diakonia* is in the developing understanding of ecclesial office. Those who share in this *diakonia* receive it as a sacred commission from another—either from the Lord himself or from those to whom he had given it earlier. *Diakon-* is indeed informing the identity of those in apostolic office, and it is reasonable to maintain it will inform the office that eventually develops as bearing the name formed from this word group, the diaconate.

DIAKON- IN THE GOSPEL OF LUKE

In the Gospel of Luke, there are three uses of *diakon-* in regards to Jesus. First, its use in Luke 12:37 is in the context of Jesus speaking to his "disciples" (cf. Luke 12:22). Here, Jesus says that it is the master who will *diakoneō* for his *douloi* (slaves). Like Mark 10:43-44, we see a connection between *diakon-* and *doulos*. Second, its use in Luke 17:8 is in the context of Jesus addressing his "apostles" (last mentioned in Luke 17:5), teaching them about how they are to conduct themselves. He uses the image of a *doulos* whose master expects them to *diakoneiv*.

Last, the most significant use of *diakon-* in reference to Jesus comes in the context of the Last Supper. Jesus uses a participle *diakonōn* (from *diakoneō*) to refer to himself (Luke 22:27) after telling the apostles that a leader ought to be "one who serves" (*diakonōn*) in the previous verse. Note the similarity to the Gospel of Mark; what Jesus does is what the apostles are to do; they are to follow in his way.[39]

DIAKON- IN LUKE 22:27

In the chapter in which he discusses *diakon-* in Jesus' ministry, Collins reasons how Luke uses *diakoneō* in the context of the Last Supper, arguing that Luke uses it intentionally.[40] First, Collins notes several indications that Luke's redaction of the scene manifests his Hellenistic background and interests by shaping the material into a Greek *symposion*; his observations follow. Jesus' words are a farewell address from the master to his disciples. Moreover, among other Hellenistic touches, Luke stresses a key aspect of the entire Gospel by emphasizing the nature of the kingdom. The verses that follow Luke 22:27 concern the dispute about greatness: "Jesus acknowledges the fidelity of the *disciples* and assures them of their place in the kingdom that his Father has assigned to him (22:28-30)."[41] Furthermore, the location of the scene in Luke is not on the roadside as in Mark (which Collins maintains Luke knew and redacted) but is in a context fitting for a symposion in which there is an esteemed host with attendants for himself and his guests.

Among Luke's Hellenistic touches to the passage, Collins also includes the presence of the *diakon-* word group, since Luke is following "Greek literary convention" and is aware of its proper meaning. Moreover, Luke also chooses to use a participial form of this word group (*diakonōn*), a grammatical form characteristic of Hellenistic literature. Collins argues that "Luke's intention is to cultivate the community's awareness of the Lord's presence in [the kingdom]. 'I am in your midst like one who is attending at the tables.' This is the point of the resolution of the dispute in Jesus's discourse. Disputes must end because the Lord is 'in the midst.'"[42] Collins argues that Luke's choice to include diakonōn "is not the result of casual usage. Nor is its presence in the narrative for the purpose of inculcating lessons about lowly service by one member of the community to another. *The only reason Luke uses the word is to contribute to the dignity of the occasion. As a minor stylistic feature, diakon- is recognizable to Luke's readers as marking the formal and religious nature of the occasion.*"[43] However, the significance of Luke's use of *diakon-* here in Luke 22 is greater than just contributing to Hellenistic stylizing; it needs to be related to his refined use of *diakonia* in Acts.

The greater significance of *diakon-* in Luke 22 is first seen from the fact that it is used in the context of the word "apostles." At the beginning of the Last Supper—the meal integral to the symposion—we have, "When the hour came, he took his place at table with the apostles" (Luke 22:14). The connection with the apostles to the Twelve in the context of the Gospel is clear (even if by the end of Acts, the definition of apostle has been expanded beyond the well-defined group), "When day came, he called his disciples to himself, and from them he chose Twelve, whom he also named apostles" (Luke 6:13). Luke is the only Gospel to use *diakon-* in the context of the Last Supper as a way to exhort what is appropriate for the group Jesus is addressing (Luke 22:26) and as a self-reference to Jesus, himself (Luke 22:27). One can argue, therefore, that Luke's intentional use of *diakon-* in his Last Supper scene relates to his use of it in Acts. Even if one grants that Luke is redacting Mark, his use here, while related to Mark, demonstrates also some intention of his own and indicates how, for Luke, the Twelve stress the importance of *diakonia* in their role in Acts 1. Moreover, its use there leads into the use of the term in Acts 6, as seen above.

Furthermore, in agreement with Collins, Luke is not just trying to teach something "about lowly service by one member of the community to another"; but, beyond supporting a *symposion*, Luke is communicating that "to be one who serves (*diakonōn*)" relates to what Jesus did on the cross, thus expressing a point quite similar to Mark 10:42-45. The relationship of Luke's *diakonōn* in Luke 22:27 to the cross is noted by Arthur A. Just:

> Jesus' ministry of service is ultimately to be understood as his atoning sacrifice, for he has just said, "This is my body, which is being given on behalf of you" (22:19) and "This cup is the new testament in my blood, which is being poured out on behalf of you" (22:20).[44]

Thus, Luke, while not having an explicit reference to Jesus' sacrificial death on the cross in Luke 22:27 like "ransom" in Mark 10:45 (and Matt 20:28), he still manifests Jesus' death on the cross in the context of the passage by a direct reference to Jesus' blood being poured out, a phrase that, while not unique to the Synoptic passion scenes, is unique in Luke as it informs his use of *diakon-*.[45]

In a related way, Just notes that "Jesus' full explanation of the significance of his death as ὁ διακονῶν (*ho diakonōn*), 'the one who serves' (22:27), is reserved for the colloquium with the Emmaus disciples in 24:25-27,"[46] in which Jesus says, "Was it not necessary that the Messiah should suffer these things and enter into his glory?" (24:26). In short, there is merit in the thought that Luke's use of *diakon-* in the Last Supper narrative relates to what Jesus does on the cross; thus, while coming in different contexts, we see clear overlap of the *diakon-* of Jesus in Mark with that in Luke.

Finally, in the verses that follow Luke 22:27, the context further demonstrates Luke's awareness of the classical sense of *diakon-*. In Luke 22:28-30, Jesus says that what was given to him by the Father he will give to the apostles. Jesus received his mission of *diakonia* from the Father, and he in turn hands it on to his apostles. If Luke's use of *diakonia* in Acts is a code word, as Collins convincingly asserts, the foundation of that use is prepared in an astute use of *diakonōn* in his account of the passion.[47]

Thus, while Collins is correct to point out that Luke's unique use of *diakon-* in the Last Supper relates to *symposion*, further significance of its use here comes from the context of Luke 22:24-27. Luke uses *diakon-* here in a way similar to Mark 10:42-45 (cf. Matt 20:25-28), that is, in the context of a dispute involving the twelve apostles in which *diakon-* ties to Jesus' sacrifice; Luke's phrase "which is being given on behalf of you" (Luke 22:19) conveys a similar sense to Mark's "ransom" (Mark 10:45).[48] Furthermore, Luke's use of *diakon-* in Luke 22:26-27 contributes to the programmatic way in which Luke uses the word group regarding the Twelve in Acts. In the Gospel of Luke, *diakonōn* speaks to Jesus' mission (Luke 22:27) to which he also calls the twelve apostles (Luke 22:26), while in Acts 1, the Twelve explicitly take up the mission of *diakonia*. Then as the narrative of Acts progresses, the use of *diakonia* broadens as the sense of apostolic ministry broadens. The first step in this broadening process takes place when the Twelve offer in a formal way a share in their *diakonia* to the seven in Acts 6 through prayer and the laying on of hands.[49] We noted earlier how Stephen, one of the recipients of a share in this *diakonia*, carries it out as a sacred commission to preach in the chapters following Acts 6. We can now note with benefit that the martyrdom of Stephen, stylized by Luke to show his union with Jesus, manifests another aspect of Stephen's *diakonia*, his sacrificial death offered after the example of Jesus.

CONCLUSION

We saw in the Gospel of Mark how Jesus is manifested as the bearer of a message from his Father who is its originator. Flowing out of this singular relationship to God, Jesus is offered as a ransom for many. Moreover, it is his weakness intrinsic to the means of his ransom that shows the power of the one who originates the message. The apostles have a particular call as *diakonoi*; they are to exercise their authority not as Gentile rulers but as *douloi* (Mark 10:42–44). They are go-betweens, receiving their commission from Jesus (Mark 3:14), to perpetuate Jesus' ransom in their words and deeds.

Having a lower rank of office than the apostles, the seven nonetheless act as go-betweens in the name of the Lord. Like the apostles, they too must have "a singular relationship to the God who originates" the message they bear. We see this singular relationship lived out in the life of the Twelve through their call to "be with [Jesus]" (Mark 3:14) and their desire to continue in "prayer and the *diakonia* of the word" (Acts 6:4). In fact, it is to enable the latter activities that the seven are called. Yet, given that the share of *diakonia* commissioned to them has them carry out similar Word-centered activities and leads to the sacrifice of Stephen's life, we see concrete overlap between their *diakonia* and that of the apostles and also that of Paul. While they have a subservient role relative to the apostles, the nature of their task and message necessitates likewise a substantial living relationship with the Lord Jesus. For in their weakness, they bear a message that is not their own.

Luke does something unique with *diakon-* in Luke 22:26-27. He places it in the eucharistic context of the Last Supper, which fits within his programmatic use of it in Acts. Luke is well aware of the contemporary meaning of this term and through it, connects the giving of Jesus' body and blood to his offering on the cross. Through carrying out his *diakonia*, Jesus is faithful to the sacred task entrusted to him by the Father. Jesus likewise confers his *diakonia* on his apostles. Moreover, we see the Twelve embrace their *diakonia* in Acts 1, which in Acts 6, they formally, through prayer and the laying on of hands, share with the seven. The explicit priority of the newly constituted is on the preaching of the Word as manifest in the activity of Stephen and Philip, while noting the overtones of the Eucharist in the *diakonia* conveyed in Acts 6. If the *diakonia* of Jesus in Luke connects to the sacrificial offering of the Last Supper fulfilled on the cross, we can likewise see eucharistic overtones in the *diakonia* of Stephen in his martyrdom. While the development of the ranks of holy orders was still in development, we cannot separate the fact that one of them took its name, well established by the time of Ignatius of Antioch, from the word group *diakon-*, the office of deacon.

Since there is lack of clarity about the specific development of ecclesiastical offices in the New Testament and yet a relationship of the various ranks to the Twelve, that is, the lower ranks share to some extent in the apostleship of the Twelve, perhaps what is most important today for those living out vocations of priesthood and diaconate is to recognize that what is spoken to the Twelve by Jesus at the time of their call applies equally to deacons; they are to be with Jesus (Mark 3:14) before they do anything. Such union with Jesus allows them to carry out the *diakonia* inherent in their vocation more faithfully as the apostles were to live out their *diakonia* in imitation of Jesus.

Based on the use of *diakon-* in the Gospels and Acts, this being with Jesus must manifest itself in faithfully carrying out the sacred commission to preach and in generously making the gift of self exemplified in Jesus' self-offering on the cross, that is, the fullest expression of the mission entrusted to him by the Father. This is the core identity of anyone who bears the office whose name comes from the word group *diakon-*. The more the priest can recognize that his call to be with Jesus in holy orders begins sacramentally from his ordination as deacon, the more he will appreciate and welcome the one whose call leads him to a permanent embrace of the diaconate.

NOTES

1. Jean Galot, *Theology of the Priesthood* (San Francisco: Ignatius Press, 2005), 169. Galot footnotes this comment with the following quotation: "The name *diakonoi* was first used to refer to all itinerant ministers, the 'apostles' included. Then it was used mostly to designate secretaries, assistants, or co-workers of the 'apostles', of Paul in particular' (Lemaire, *Les Ministères*, p. 198)" (Galot, 175).

2. Galot, *Theology of the Priesthood*, 170.

3. Specifically, *diakonia, diakoneō, diakonos*, that is, that which makes up the *diakon-* word group. Cf. John N. Collins, *Diakonia Studies: Critical Issues in Ministry* (New York: Oxford University Press, 2014), 78.

4. Cf. Catholic Church, *From the diakonia of Christ to the diakonia of the Apostles: Historico-Theological Research Document* (Chicago: Hillenbrand Books, 2003), 83.

5. Galot, *Priesthood*, 74.

6. Ibid., 73.

7. Ibid., 74.

8. Ibid.

9. *Diakon-* as table service is the prevalent definition in scholarship, for example, "The original meaning of *diakonein* is 'to wait on, to serve at table,' and, in contrast to all other Greek words denoting service, it emphasizes the personal nature of the service performed, and the character of the service as a service of love (so Bayer, in *Theologisches Wörterbuch zum Neuen Testament*, ed. G. Kittel, II, p. 81)" in John Amedee Bailey, *The Traditions Common to the Gospels of Luke and John* (Leiden: Brill, 1963), 34–35n2. Such a footnote is an example of how *diakon-* came to be so incorrectly understood as described at

length by Collins in chapter 1, "The Latter-Day Servant Church," John N. Collins, *Diakonia: Re-interpreting the Ancient Sources* (New York: Oxford University Press, 1990), 5–45; and in "Part One: Diakonia from the Nineteenth Century to Today," Collins, *Diakonia Studies*, 3–53.

10. Collins, *Diakonia*, 194, emphasis mine.
11. Ibid., 207.
12. Ibid., 209–10.
13. Collins, *Diakonia Studies*, 118.
14. For the nontechnical reader, both uses of *diakon-* here in Mark 10:45 are infinitives of *diakoneō*, the first is passive and the second is active. At the beginning of his discussion of Mark 10:45, Collins gives a free translation of the verse as a subtitle to the subsection, "The Son of Man came to carry out his mission and give his life as a ransom for many" (Collins, *Diakonia Studies*, 79).
15. Collins, *Diakonia*, 251.
16. Ibid., 252. Moreover, Collins mentions how in "to serve and give his life as a ransom for many," the "and" serves epexegetically, "to serve, that is, to give his life as a ransom for many" (Collins, *Diakonia Studies*, 83).
17. Collins, *Diakonia Studies*, 83.
18. Ibid.
19. Ibid.
20. Ibid.
21. Francis J. Moloney, *The Gospel of Mark: A Commentary* (Peabody, MA: Hendrickson Publishers, 2002), 208.
22. Collins, *Diakonia Studies*, 157–58.
23. Catholic Biblical Association (Great Britain), *The Holy Bible: Revised Standard Version, Catholic Edition* (New York: National Council of Churches of Christ in the USA, 1994), Acts 1:8.
24. Collins, *Diakonia Studies*, 160.
25. Ibid.
26. Ibid.
27. Collins, *Diakonia Studies*, 156. N.b., Collins only says here that they rededicated themselves to the *diakonia*/ministry of the Word without explicit mention of prayer. Acts 6:4 says they rededicate themselves to "prayer" and *diakonia* of the word. "Prayer" is noteworthy given how Luke shows its prominence in the life of Jesus (e.g., Luke 3:21; 5:16; 6:12; 9:18, 28; 11:1, 22:41, 44) from whom they received the commission. The apostles would rededicate themselves to this part of Jesus' life. Moreover, prayer is a particular way that they would now, post ascension, be with Jesus (cf. Mark 3:14).
28. Collins, *Diakonia Studies*, 156.

29. "Rededicate" (from *proskartereō*) here could be translated as simply "busy oneself with, be busily engaged in, be devoted to" the activity mentioned (with dative of thing, BDAG προσκαρτερέω, 2.a.) as if it could be a new activity, but given the context of Acts 5:42, it is better here to take it as Collins does above, "hold fast to, continue in, persevere in" (with dative of thing, BDAG προσκαρτερέω, 2.b.), that is, "rededicate." BDAG = William Arndt, Frederick W. Danker, and Walter Bauer, *A Greek-English Lexicon of the New Testament and Other Early Christian Literature* (Chicago: University of Chicago Press, 2000), 492.

30. The common understanding today of the "*diakonein* at table."

31. Collins, *Diakonia Studies*, 160-161. See also Galot, *Priesthood*, 161-63, who in addition, speaks of Philip's (and the rest of the seven's) work as eucharistic.

32. *Euaggelizō* occurs ten times in Luke and fifteen times in Acts while only occurring once in Matthew and not appearing at all in both Mark and John.

33. Some scholars hold that the "breaking of the bread" of Acts 2:42 was simply a common meal shared by the early Christian community (e.g., Barclay M. Newman and Eugene A. Nida, *A Handbook on the Acts of the Apostles*, UBS Handbook Series [New York: United Bible Societies, 1972], 63). Yet both Catholic and Protestant biblical scholarship recognizes that this act needs to be something more than a common meal because of its connection to Luke 24:35, the only other use of this phrase, where there is an association between the "breaking of the bread" and Jesus' resurrected presence (so Luke T. Johnson, *The Acts of the Apostles*, ed. Daniel J. Harrington, vol. 5, Sacra Pagina Series [Collegeville, MN: The Liturgical Press, 1992], 58) or because of its link to "what came to be called the Lord's Supper" and the "breaking" of Jesus' body in death (so F. F. Bruce, *The Book of the Acts*, The New International Commentary on the New Testament [Grand Rapids, MI: Eerdmans, 1988], 73).

34. Galot, *Priesthood*, 161-62; Galot goes on to argue that given the eucharistic overtones here that the seven should be considered "presbyters," leaving that designation in quotations marks saying that "we should bear in mind that at the beginning the term 'presbyter' is used without precision" (Galot, 163).

35. Ibid., 163.

36. Collins, *Diakonia*, 212.

37. Collins, *Diakonia Studies*, 158. Besides these uses that in some way refer to the apostles or to Paul (namely, Acts 1:17, 25; 6:1,

2, 4; 20:24; 21:19), there are just three others. These uses, while not part of Luke's programmatic use of *diakonia* as described by Collins, still fall within his renewed definition of *diakon-*. Moreover, the first two involve Saul and Barnabas dispatching the *diakonia* collected by others for the Church in Jersalem (Acts 11:29) and is used to describe their *diakonia* together (Acts 12:25). It is worth noting that the second of these follows a sort of summary verse relating to the spread of the "word of God" (Acts 11:24). Last, the third use of *diakon-* comes from a participle of *diakoneō*—the only use of *diakon-* in Acts (besides Acts 6:2: *diakonein* at table) that is not *diakonia*—to refer to "two assistants/ministers," that is, Timothy and Erastus (Act 19:22).

38. The last two remaining uses of *euaggelizō* have as their subject God himself (Acts 10:36) and the Cypriots and Cyrenians who come to Antioch to preach in Greek (Acts 11:20). These latter *proclaimers* incidentally were among those who had been scattered by the persecution of Stephen (Acts 11:19).

39. It is not unlike the use of *euaggelizō* in regards to Jesus and the apostles (Luke 9:6; cf. 8:1). As mentioned above, the *euaggelizō* that Jesus does is the *euaggelizō* that the apostles do, which is instructive for its use in Acts.

40. Collins, *Diakonia Studies*, 88-94.

41. Ibid., 91, emphasis mine—I will show presently that it would be more precise to use *apostles* in this context.

42. Ibid., 93.

43. Ibid., emphasis mine.

44. Arthur A. Just, *Luke 9:51–24:53* (St. Louis: Concordia Publishing House, 1997), 846n9.

45. Arthur A. Just references in part J. Fitzmyer, who demonstrates that Luke expresses God's salvific plan as coming through Jesus' suffering and death. Luke is unique in the extent that he presents Jesus as the Messiah who "must suffer" (9:22; 17:25; 24:7). Moreover, Luke further depicts Jesus as "the prophet aware that he has to perish in Jerusalem (Luke 13:33)....In other words, the Lucan 'necessity' involved in the plan of salvation-history has a bearing on the death of Jesus" (Joseph A. Fitzmyer, *The Gospel According to Luke I-IX* [Garden City, NY: Doubleday, 1981], 220).

46. Just, *Luke*, 846n9.

47. Moreover, thinking of the meaning of *diakon-* articulated so well in Collins work, we see important aspects of its meaning in the life of Jesus and the apostles in Luke even though the explicit use *diakon-* is lacking: Jesus receives all things from his Father (Luke 10:22; cf. Matt 11:27); He possesses authority (Luke 4:32; 5:24—as in

Matthew and Mark); and Jesus gives the Twelve authority (Luke 9:1). See also Galot's comment on Luke 22:28-30, "Disposing of the kingdom in favor of the Twelve is tantamount to imparting to them total power: Jesus, who has received this power from the Father, bestows it upon his apostles....But Luke also stresses the connection between the power conferred upon the Twelve and the commitment to sacrifice. Jesus disposes of the kingdom in favor of those who have stood by him faithfully in his trials. Thus a new similarity comes to the fore. Jesus had described his pastoral power by positing a relation between it and sacrifice. This connection perdures in the disciples" (Galot, *Priesthood*, 76). For Galot, this connection is tied closely to the celebration of the Eucharist given the context of the Last Supper here.

48. While Luke does not use the explicit term for sacrificial death as in Mark 10:45, "ransom," "it would be a mistake to conclude that Luke does not ascribe redemptive significance to Jesus' death. The immediate purpose of the saying in Luke 22:27 is to present Jesus as the servant model for the exercise of authority in the community. The redemptive power of Jesus' death has already been proclaimed loud and clear in the scene in the words over the bread and the cup. Given that context, it is also clear that the image of 'servant' applies to Jesus' death. Offering his life for others is Jesus' ultimate act of table service, that is, it has redemptive significance." Donald Senior, *The Passion of Jesus in the Gospel of Luke* (Wilmington, DE: M. Glazier, 1989), 70-71.

49. See also Marion Soards's brief comment on Luke 22:27a-d, "While it certainly is no longer possible to deny the presence of sacrificial nuance in Luke's Gospel, the emphasis here is on the *service of Jesus*. Jesus *serves* by giving his body and pouring out his blood." Emphasis in original. Marion L. Soards, *The Passion According to Luke: The Special Material of Luke 22* (Sheffield: JSOT Press, 1987), 51.

2.

The Mystery of Jesus as Deacon

STEPHEN F. MILETIC

THE CHALLENGE

At first glance, the Gospel of Mark[1] appears to be void of anything regarding the deacon as a formal, public (ordained) minister of the Church, unlike other New Testament texts (e.g., 1 Tim 3:8, 12, etc.). The primary focus of this first-century narrative is to present the identity and saving mission of Jesus Christ, Son of God (Mark 1:1; 15:39). Jesus announces the presence of the gospel of God and that the "time of salvation" is now fully present in a sustained fashion (1:15a).[2] This is a call to repentance (conversion of mind, a transformed mind, *metanoeite*),[3] and a commanding summons to faith (*pisteuete*). There is nothing explicit about the diaconate. Unfortunately, as we will note below, the quantitative data for the *diakon-* word complex[4] is small. Furthermore, the Greek noun for "service" or "ministry" (*diakonia*) does not even occur in the Gospel. These three factors would seem to militate against any attempt at probing the Gospel for diaconal sacramental identity.[5]

Consequently, we will argue that in the Gospel of Mark, (1) Christ is the *sacrament of God*, (2) Mark's presentation of Christ's self-understanding and his salvific mission is cast in the form of salvific *service*, and (3) Christ *transfers* his sacramentally configured salvific service to the apostles and other followers. Moreover, in light of Mark's narrative, we will examine what lies at the core of diaconal sacramental identity.

SACRAMENT AND SACRED TRADITION[6]

Before exploring the Gospel, let us first consider the nature of a sacrament. The *Catechism of the Catholic Church* provides a convenient starting point for understanding a sacrament:

> The sacraments are *efficacious signs of grace*, instituted by Christ and entrusted to the church, *by which divine life is dispensed to us*. The *visible rites* by which the sacraments are celebrated *signify and make present* the graces proper to each sacrament. They bear fruit in those who receive them with the required dispositions. (§113)[7]

And later, we read:

> Celebrated worthily in faith, the *sacraments confer* the grace that they signify. They are efficacious because in them *Christ himself is at work*: it is he who baptizes, *he who acts in his sacraments* in order to *communicate the grace* that each sacrament signifies. (§1127)

A sacrament *signifies* and *makes present God, Divine Life* ("graces proper to each sacrament"). Christ is the source of the Church's sacraments "because in them Christ himself is at work"; he acts in and communicates through the grace signified by particular sacramental signs. We may note the complete identity between the spiritual, invisible source of the sacrament—Christ—and its material means of mediation—Divine Life working through the sacramental signs. Spiritual realities are known through their material signs.[8]

Here, we are particularly interested in how the narrative articulates the sacramental realities of Jesus. In fact, the Gospel *progressively* reveals Jesus as the Anointed One, the Son of God, and Son of Man. Together, these three elements present a Markan understanding of Jesus as the sacrament of God; his identity and saving mission express a Markan sacramental character. In other words, Jesus' identity and mission are the foundation of the diaconal sacramental character.

CHRIST, THE SACRAMENT OF GOD

"Whoever welcomes me welcomes not me but the one who sent me." (Mark 9:37 NRSV)

If Christ is the sacrament of God,[9] then God is the root of "sacramental grace" (Divine Life) flowing through Christ. Given the inseparable unity between sacramental source and sign—God and Christ—our first task is to detect where in the Gospel of Mark we find indications of the unity of God and Christ. This, in turn, will assist our reflection on the phenomenon of sacramental identity and presence in the Gospel.

The following passages are particularly relevant expressions of Jesus' unity with God. In Markan terms, they express an understanding of unity between God and Jesus. They are also applicable to the entire narrative world.[10] Typically, the thematic content of a passage is stated and then sometimes repeated to reinforce and deepen previous statements by revealing new dimensions previously hidden to the reader.[11] For example, the combination of "Son of God" plus "Son of Man" introduces the essence of a servant-character to the notion of Son of God. Consequently, it is not apparent from Mark 1:1 that the term, "Son of God," is linked to a servant role, Son of Man; it is a mystery hidden in the reality of Jesus that needs to be revealed in later events of the narrative. Therefore, these passages furnish major narratological clues assisting the reader/hearer to grasp the global statement of the narrative.[12]

The Christ and Son of God

Mark 1:1 NRSV: "The beginning of the good news of Jesus Christ, the Son of God."[13] The "title verse" proclaims the central mystery of God: Jesus, the Anointed, is Son of God. This proclamation is the first example of a global statement. It applies to the whole of the narrative. It has three functions. First, it introduces the entire Gospel as a narrative; the kind of story about Jesus—the literary genre: Gospel. Second, it introduces the kind of content that the Son of God brings forth. In first-century Mediterranean culture, "Son of God" often means "one who has the essential characteristics and nature of God."[14] Hence, this narrative is a literary presentation (gospel) about Divine good news (however understood at this early portion of the narrative). Then, in Mark 1:4, the message of repentance and forgiveness of sins introduced by John the Baptist begins to reveal the meaning of the term "good news" or "gospel," and later in Mark 2, when Jesus forgives sins, the understanding of the term is transformed by becoming a precursor to Jesus' ministry for the forgiveness of sins. Third, the application of both titles "Anointed One" (Christ) and "Son of God" to Jesus within a "global" statement signifies a special "closeness" to God in both mission and identity that applies throughout the Gospel. The relationship between these two terms is progressively developed throughout the narrative.[15]

Mark 1:9–12: Christ (Anointed One) is the Son of God. This passage is yet another global statement, which now associates Jesus' anointing by the Spirit with God's Divine affirmation: "You are my Son, the Beloved" (Mark 1:11 NRSV).

The context and literary features of chapter 1 lead us to the conclusion that the Father *sends* or causes three works of salvation. We see this emerge through the missions of the Baptist, the Spirit, and Jesus, respectively. The Father *sends* John the Baptist (Mark1:2–3)[16] to baptize all Jerusalem and Judea (1:5), and Jesus (1:9). He sends the Spirit (1:10) and will *send* the Son[17] through the newly present Spirit (1:10, 13) to proclaim the good news (1:14–15).

At Jesus' baptism, the Father "tears open"[18] the heavens (v. 10a) and *sends* the Spirit to descend on the Son, thus anointing him (v. 10b). Next, the Father speaks directly to his Son, almost as a commentary on Jesus' immersion in the Spirit—the anointed Jesus is "my Son, the Beloved [only]; with you I am well pleased" (1:11). The phrase "my Son, the Beloved" signals the next development of Jesus' special identity and unique closeness to the Father that was initially presented in verse 1. The term, "Beloved" (*agapētos*), which means "only son" in the Old Testament (LXX)[19] underscores not only filial intimacy but a unique and exclusive relationship. Jesus, the Son, receives the Spirit, who publically identifies him as the Anointed, but is also proclaimed as Son by God (v. 11). The anointed humanity of Jesus is not like that of past kings or prophets;[20] it is as one who is the only Son. The mystery of the Father's intimate presence in the Son, signaled by Divine speech, affirms Jesus Christ in a unique filial way. Jesus is the sacrament of God.[21]

In other words, the Divine sending (causality) of the Baptist, the Spirit, and Divine speech all conspire to signal God's presence in the historical figure of Jesus through an exclusive and substantial relationship with God—one of *filial* intimacy distinguishable and *unique* from any other. The one points to the other and to the closeness between the two. The Son makes present the Father; he is the sacrament of God.

The Kenotic Jesus

Mark 1:14-15. Again we have a global statement—the dominant theme of the narrative—and a new development of a quality of Jesus' historical existence.[22] He comes as one *sent* by God to announce something about God. The anointed Son announces *neither his own gospel nor his own kingdom*. On the contrary, Jesus announces someone ("of God") and something ("good news," "kingdom") other than himself. This implied filial deference to the Father marks Jesus' implied kenotic or self-emptied status as the unique Son.[23] Mark does not use the term *kenosis*—a state of being self-emptied—but it will be confirmed in Jesus' prayer to the Father in the Garden of Gethsemane (Mark 14:34-39) and when he prays Psalm 22 just before his death (Mark 15:34). The drama of the narrative's theocentric focus and the fact that Jesus *does not preach his own gospel* but rather mediates God's presence makes him the sacrament of God.

Jesus, God's Sacrament of Healing and Forgiveness

Mark 2:1-12. Our final example of a global statement escalates Jesus' identity to an explicit sacramental identity. The story is as follows: Jesus preaches the "word" (of God) (2:2); men bring a paraplegic expecting to be healed by Jesus (2:3-4); the anticipated healing is interrupted and delayed when Jesus recognizes their faith and forgives the man's sins (2:5); the scribes' interior reactions indirectly challenge Jesus' exercise of the divine prerogative to forgive sins (2:7), and finally, the Son of Man then heals the man as a sign of his exercise of divine authority to forgive sins (2:10-11).

Given the narrative's linear development to this point, one would have expected the "Anointed Son of God" to have authority and power to forgive sins "from his own being" (*exousia*).[24] And yet Jesus identifies himself as the "Son of Man."[25] Why? The humanity of the "Son of Man" mediates the Father's forgiveness. The Son of Man's authority could certainly be "from his own being" but that is as the Son unified with the Father, the Son whose kenotic character is in filial deference to the Father. His unity with the Father does not lessen his identity and divinity as Son when he self-presents as Son of Man. It expresses deference to the Father who authorizes. The phase, then, makes it possible for the Son of Man to be fully engaged, responsible for his human task while not lessening his unity with the Father and divine status as Son of God. On *mission for another*, the Son of Man is the servant of the Father bringing God's "good news" of healing, forgiveness of sins, and the commanding summons to faith in God. Christologically, the work is enacted but theologically—God the Father—driven. In Markan terms, the Son of Man is the sacramental presence of the Son of God, who makes God's "good news" and "kingdom" present through healing and forgiveness.

Conclusions

Therefore, guided by the global statements and events about Jesus' identity and mission in the Gospel of Mark, we come to understand that Jesus mediates the divine presence of God. There is an inseparable bond between sign (Jesus) and what he signifies (God). The relationship between the sacramental character of Jesus and the Servant Mysteries becomes clearer as we examine the *diakon-* word complex.

CHRIST'S SERVANT MYSTERIES

Like the "global" passages just reviewed, the vocabulary of the *diakon-* word complex strategically connects service with Jesus' salvific mission. These texts are connected to salvation by way of their association with Mark 10:45, the primary source fusing service with salvation. Additionally, these texts intend to engender, provoke, or otherwise elicit a faith response from the reader. Given this inherent dynamic of the narrative, contemplative reflections from the twenty-first century constitute an essential role in understanding how this Gospel sheds light on the sacramental identity of the deacon.

Jesus Overcomes Satan (1:12-13)

Immediately after his baptism, Jesus is driven into the desert to be "tested."[26] After his forty-day test, an angel ministers (*diēkonoun*) to Jesus in the presence of wild animals (1:13). The association of "test" with wilderness and forty days evokes many Old Testament themes, like that of Moses' desert fast for purification (Deut 9:18; cf. Exod 34:28) and Elijah's fast in the desert at the foot to Mount Horeb (1 Kgs 19:8), possibly the notion of Israel's betrothal to God in the desert and the wilderness as the locus of revelation. Each of these instances suggests a time of preparation prior to a divinely commissioned mission. The angelic ministry to Jesus recalls that the desert was also a place of rebellion against God, full of threats to human life from the environment and from wild beasts, and the "residence" of demonic power. Why did the Son of God, the Anointed One, need ministry from angels?[27]

These verses present another example of the kenotic Son of God who relies completely on God for mission. The many examples of Old Testament figures who relied on God for their mission and subsistence, out of obedience to God, are numerous. Abraham responds to the Divine charge to leave his father's house and go to a place that God will reveal to him (Gen 12:1ff.). He is willing to offer in sacrifice his only son at God's request (Gen 22:1ff.). In such cases, angels are not at play, but there is a theological and spiritual parallel. Abraham's obedience expresses a kenotic disposition of discharging his own thought, life, and desires for those of God—to pursue God's will. If so, then Abraham's faith—his kenotic disposition—appears to anticipate a similar disposition expressed by Jesus' reception of angelic ministry in our passage. This is an implied kenotic, filial deference to God's ways of providing, as he has with Ancient Israel. He relies not on self for food, but on the ministry of the Father's "sent ones"—the meaning of "angels."[28] This kenotic existence is further echoed when he prays Psalm 22 on the cross (Mark 15:34), a prayer of complete surrender to God. Jesus the Son of God, in Markan terms, is the Son of Man, the faithful suffering servant who overcomes evil.

Contemplative Reflection

The Spirit *sends* the anointed Son of God into the wilderness to be tested. Paradoxically, he appears to vanquish Satan as a weak human being. He suffers the threat of wild beasts and of human want (one of the Markan points about the angels and beasts). The Father sustains him. Diaconal filial obedience to the Spirit's prompting confronts us with our own evil (human and spiritual), that of others, and with the demonic powers that make it worse. Our sacramental character is our bond with the tired, thirsty, hungry Christ. Through that bond, we learn about our own kenosis, our dependency on God. In our interior desert, we learn docility to the Spirit, who can then send us to external places of desolation, depression, and discouragement; to the human deserts of our families, parishes, and dioceses. When we identify with the desolation of Christ and those whom God sends us, we learn about the ministry of sacrificial love. Existentially, we become more the "son" we became at ordination as we bring the Son to any "poor." We are Christ's sacrament of loving service leading to redemption.

Other uses of the verbal forms of the *diakon-* word complex associate the term with Jesus' power over physical evil, also expressed in terms of salvific service as discussed below.

Healing Leads to Service (1:29-31)

Jesus is told about Peter's mother-in-law's fever and heals her. She rises up and serves them. This passage presents a dramatic encounter between the power of physical evil and God's kingdom. The drama focuses on Jesus' actions. The verb describing Jesus' healing of the mother-in-law, "to take," suggests an extended or sustained force (so as to be able to lift her up). One paraphrase could be, "he continuously holds [but does not crush] her hand and simultaneously[29] "raised her up."[30] In powerful language, Jesus' sustained hold of her hand is like a direct confrontation with an evil power (fever), forcing that evil power "to release, let go of its grip on her" (*aphiēmi*).

Contemplative Reflection

The fruit of Christ's healing touch relieves suffering, frees up the bound, and leads to service to Christ and the kingdom of God. In spiritual terms, healing is not complete until it unfolds into the service of another. Significantly, it is a ministry directed to Jesus and to his Church. Jesus' healing—the *sacrament of God*—bears a diaconal fruit in a woman (divinely restored health that breaks the power of evil over us: the inclination to self-centeredness that any serious sickness brings) and empowers ministry to the other. Jesus' diaconal ministry to the Church—the mother-in-law and so all of us—expresses a diaconal grace "caught" by Peter's mother-in-law. Divinely healed, she embodies the Church's ministry to Jesus, the Church, and others in need.

Service Defines Ecclesial Leadership (9:33-37)

The followers of Jesus are discussing who would be the greatest of them all, and when asked by Jesus about their discussion, they could not reply (9:33). Sitting down (v. 35), Jesus summons the Twelve to explain what "first" means for the kingdom. Jesus begins by "sitting down." The participle could signal either someone assuming a seat of authoritative power (e.g., Jesus at God's right hand, Eph 1:20; Moses' seat of teaching authority, Matt 23:2) or just sitting down. Here, both seem applicable. In the sitting position, Jesus makes an authoritative pronouncement: the one wishing to be "first" in God's kingdom must be or become "servant of all." And yet, servants do not sit on seats of authority. Could Jesus' posture itself be like an "enacted" parable, demonstrative, performing "first" from the position of a child whom he is next to receive (Mark 9:36-37)? Jesus acts out what he says. Jesus sits as a servant, a child, as he teaches authoritatively about servant-leadership.

Contemplative Reflection

This historical Jesus is humble, a servant. His diaconal character's end game is to let God's life and presence flow throughout his being and ministry, which will save us when he is completely emptied of human life on his cross. His embodiment of diaconal service, then, has a salvific purpose. As with Christ's emptied, weakened, suffering humanity at the cross, so deacon candidates present themselves at their ordinations, prostrate on the floor, bodily invoking a prayer spoken out loud in the rite, prayed by the candidates from the heart, "Lord, have mercy." Through no effort of his own—the gift of sacramental reconfigurement, the position of laying prostrate on the floor, invoking the help of God, the saints, and the angels—the deacon candidate is lower than sitting—"all laid out," "all committed"—and in being so, rises and receives the gift of the Spirit through the bishop. The deacon is reconfigured to Christ the Servant, bonded with him in the soul, now one with the Servant. Deacons rise to receive this transformation of the Spirit, but our interior posture must remain "all laid out." Our prayer is for the deepest humility. What appears as a descent is in reality an ascent into the heart of our brother Deacon, our Lord and Savior.

Let us consider two more specific instances of the *diakon-* word complex. The first is another example of the diaconal character of ecclesial service (Jesus' female followers) and the other presents the identity and mission of Jesus.

Servant-Discipleship in the Church (15:40-41)

We are at Jesus' crucifixion. Mary Magdalene, Mary the mother of James the younger and of Joses, and Salome "followed" and "ministered" to Jesus during his Galilean ministry. They have not abandoned him but have "followed" him to the cross. The association of "to follow"[31] with "acts of service" signifies the close association between following Jesus and service in these women who represent the rest of the Church.[32]

Like Peter's mother-in-law, these women received no explicit mandate to serve; but like her, they chose to serve Christ. This pattern of kenotic service of Christ is characteristic of the whole Church—all of Jesus' followers.

Contemplative Reflection

Who are these women? In the text, they have no dialogue, but we know them through the eyes of the narrator; their discipleship and service is a mystery. What does it take for a deacon to follow and serve Christ? The women's presence tells us to serve and follow Jesus right through to the Cross! The women had to be free, unfettered, unbound to follow Jesus. They—the mother, the sinner, the forgiven—put their own personal agenda aside, like Christ, living a kenotic existence as disciples. Without freedom and love, kenosis is a prison; obedience is tyranny and bondage without a true personal knowledge of Jesus. They said to a "Someone" and not to a principle or moral code, and that "Someone" healed and forgave, bringing them love and freedom. All of this is without apostolic mandate. What faith, courage, freedom; what servant-discipleship and grace! These servant-disciples, these laywomen help point the deacon to Jesus and the Cross.

The Service of Salvific Death (15:35-45)

Our final example is the most significant use of the *daikon-*word complex, unveiling Jesus' self-understanding of identity and mission.

In Mark 15:35-45, Jesus journeys to Jerusalem to be crucified. On three occasions, Jesus informs the Twelve that he will be crucified and then rise from the dead (8:31; 9:31; 10:34; cf. 9:9). Our text follows the last prediction (10:32-34). The apostles, completely clueless about what was just said, inquire about seats of future glory (10:37). In response, Jesus calls the Twelve to himself (10:32, 42) to contrast glory and power among "the Gentiles" (10:32) with that of God's kingdom (10:43-45). The antithetical parallels make his point emphatic. Gentiles exercise socioeconomic, legal, and military authority by domination, "ruling/lording it over" their subordinates. In sharp contrast, the double pairings of the kingdom's "great" with "servant" and the "being first" with "being a slave" (10:43-44) completely reverses the notion of power, greatness, and glory. These wisdom-like parings provide the interpretive context for the Son of Man coming to serve and giving over himself as a ransom for many (10:45).[33]

"Son of Man" and "Son of God"

In Mark's context, "Son of Man"[34] configures Jesus' historical ministry and salvific death as a suffering *service*.[35] The Son of Man "covers" the "Son of God's" ministry in *service*.[36] The Father, Spirit, and Son are mediated through the Son of Man who embodies the "God of Israel." The term "Son of God," then, is reserved for the strategic disclosure of that deeper identity, beyond that of miracle worker (Mark 1:1, 11; 3:11; 9:7; 12:6; 15:39).

In Mark, the Son of Man embodies the God of Israel[37] and mediates divine works, as seen by the number of divine prerogatives exercised by the Son of Man. The Son of Man pronounces the forgiveness of sins (2:10); is Lord of the Sabbath, making him equal to God (2:28); behaves as if omniscient, knowing the thoughts of men (2:8); knows his own future—passion and death (8:31; 9:31; 10:33); will return postresurrection in glory and exercise divine judgment (8:38; 14:62); will exercise great power and manifest heavenly glory (9:8-9; 13:26); fulfills Scripture (14:21); is "handed over," leading to redemptive death (14:41); and finally, is disclosed as Son of God by an imperial agent[38] (15:39) at the peak moment of salvation: his death at the cross. Jesus of Nazareth, Christ, Son of God, is Savior-Servant Son of Man. He is Deacon-Savior, Son of God.

Contemplative Reflection

Diaconal ministry is the work of Christ—Son of Man, Son of God. It must serve "unto salvation." Just as Jesus "comes to serve and give over himself as a ransom for many," our ministry must repeat that servant mystery in our existence (existentially) and work. We become a ransom when we give of our gifts of love, understanding, wisdom, and insight, all of it drawn from Christ through our renewed minds. We offer ourselves as Christ on the cross and bring the merits of his work already in us through the work of the priest to the poor and marginalized. Our service is not sufficient if it is reduced to social service. We bring the fullness of Christ to them, mediated through the sign of our own bodies and souls, like the Son of Man's humanity—his love, compassion, desire to set free, and lift up. We also are a bridge to Christ the Head; we can bring lost souls to Jesus' family, the Church, where they can become family as well. All of this is the fruit of the cross.

Finally, the Son of Man is the "outward appearance" ("bread" of the consecrated Eucharist) to the "interior substance" (the substance of "body, blood, soul, and divinity"). Deacons represent one aspect of the Son of Man—his sacred service, through the ministry of Word, liturgy, and charity. This is our "bread." Our prayer is that Jesus as Servant indwells more deeply and reaches full stature within us so that we become the "bread of life" for "the many" in all that we do and say.

DIACONAL SACRAMENTAL IDENTITY

There are many issues related to the deacon's sacramental identity and mission.[39] Through this brief study of the Gospel of Mark, we have seen that Jesus' identity and mission have a decidedly diaconal character, and that Jesus mediates God's divine life and directly informs the identity and mission of the deacon. Furthermore, the Son of Man's sacramental presence, as the sacrament of God, is the source of diaconal grace, identity, and mission. It is not quite true that there is no deacon in the Gospel of Mark; the deacon is the Deacon, Jesus Christ, Son of God.

Personal Reflections

Let us conclude with some personal reflections about diaconal identity. These personal reflections echo what has already been revealed in the Gospel of Mark and track my spiritual development as a man and deacon.

The spiritual dimension of life is the foundational power that integrates human, intellectual, and pastoral dimensions of diaconal existence and ministry.[40] Authentic humanity is always and necessarily spiritually grounded. Furthermore, diaconal spirituality originates in the liturgy and points to service in the church and world.

One aspect of diaconal identity and mission that has particularly touched my life is that of intercessor. At liturgy, I intone the Church's deepest needs for mercy and forgiveness along with interceding for the Church and world at the Universal Prayer. No matter who is present—priest, bishop, cardinal, pope—as deacon, I must intercede for others.

After ordination, something new was emerging within me. Whenever I asked how people were doing—at home, at work, in the parish, and so on—my instinct told me to pray for what they mentioned, quickly, briefly, silently. Something had changed. I became aware of myself as being on mission, and a sacred one at that! What a surprise.

Then there was the existential, experiential development. The joy and happiness in being able to care for someone in a hidden, silent way raised my spirits to a great sense of privilege—entrustment—of being "let in" to someone's life. Later, I realized, that it was "Jesus in me" acting through me for the benefit of others. The peaceful confidence that God the Father was hearing this prayer for that person and was already on the move, enabled me to trust God for any and all outcomes, of which there was no doubt in my heart.

Finally, there is the liturgical development. It wasn't until much later that I recognized the connection between the diaconal grace of intercessory prayer and the deacon's ministry of Mass. However, it was not through the intoning of the Kyrie or praying the Universal Prayers. Rather, it was through lifting up the cup by the side of the priest: "I will lift up the cup of salvation and call on the name of the Lord" (Ps 116:13 NRSV). While the Priest intoned, "Through Him, with Him, and in Him. In The Unity of the Holy Spirit…" I began to place into the chalice all the petitions that came to mind along with those I had forgotten but God had not. Much later, I connected also the Kyrie and Universal Prayer.

The liturgy is the foundation of our sacred mission in the world. The permanent deacon stabilizes Jesus servant-ministry; he embodies a permanent witness to Christ the Servant; he actualizes through the sign of his embodied personhood the ministry of Christ the Servant both within and outside the Church. May Jesus Christ be praised!

NOTES

1. For convenience's sake, the term *Gospel* refers to the narrative and *Mark* as the one responsible for the canonical shape of the final text.

2. In this instance, "the time" (the awaited time of salvation: *kairos*) has now been made present and so is fulfilled and continuously present in Jesus of Nazareth (Mark 1:15a).

3. The compound verb (*metanoeite*) literally means having a "new or second mind," after taking a second look. See Ceslas Spicq and James D. Ernest, *Theological Lexicon of the New Testament* (Peabody, MA: Hendrickson, 1994), 2:472.

The Mystery of Jesus as Deacon

4. Verb ("to serve"): Mark 1:13, 31; 10:45; 15:41; noun ("servant"): Mark 9:35; 10:43. The term is used by Collin's groundbreaking work on the diaconate. See John N. Collins, *Diakonia: Re-Interpreting the Ancient Sources* (New York, NY: Oxford University Press, 1990).

5. A fourth conundrum is the long-held theological and dogmatic proposition that all the seven sacraments were intended and instituted directly by Christ. Discussion of this issue is beyond the scope of this paper. A competent treatment of the long history to this question can be found in Bernard Leeming, *Principles of Sacramental Theology* (London/Westminster, MD: Longmans/Newman Press, 1960). See especially the discussion titled "Principle XII: A Sacrament of the New Law Cannot be Defined without Including the Immediate Institution of It by Christ," 396ff.

6. There is an organic link between ST and SS: "For both of them, flowing from the same divine wellspring, in a certain way merge into a unity and tend toward the same end." See Catholic Church, *Dei Verbum: Dogmatic Constitution on Divine Revelation*, St. Paul Edition (Boston, MA: Daughters of St. Paul, 1966), §9. (Hereafter DV). There is an organic unity of the whole (of ST and SS), see Joseph Cardinal Ratzinger and Christoph von Schönborn, *Introduction to the Catechism of the Catholic Church* (San Francisco: Ignatius Press, 1994). Hence, there is a hermeneutic of continuity between SS and ST, see chapter 7: "The Message of the Parables," in Pope Benedict XVI, *Jesus of Nazareth*, trans. Adrian J. Walker (New York: Doubleday, 2007), 183–217.

7. Catholic Church, *Catechism of the Catholic Church*, 2nd ed. (Vatican City/Washington, DC: Libreria Editrice Vaticana (distributed by United States Catholic Conference, 2000), (Hereafter CCC.)

8. See chapter 7: "The Message of the Parables," in Benedict XVI, *Jesus of Nazareth*, 183–217.

9. The majority of seminal Markan scholarship over the past thirty years vigorously rejects any notion that Jesus is an embodiment of the God of Israel. For a review of literature and a robust rebuttal, see Joshua E. Leim, "In the Glory of His Father: Intertextuality and the Apocalyptic Son of Man in the Gospel of Mark," *Journal of Theological Interpretation* 7, no. 1 (2013): 213–32.

10. This is the literary reality generated by any kind of story: a joke, biography, myth, and epic. A narrative world carries its own assumptions about reality, how reality works (whether in history or fiction).

11. So we are not referring to a hermeneutic of "words interpreting words" but of words manifesting, opening up, spiritual realities. See Carbajosa, "The Nature of Exegesis and The Methodological Dimensions of Exegesis," 151–58, esp. 156, as well as the literature

cited in Ignacio Carbajosa, *Faith, the Fount of Exegesis: The Interpretation of Scripture in the Light of the History of Research on the Old Testament*, trans. Paul Stevenson (San Francisco, CA: Ignatius Press, 2013).

12. Most of the examples are from Mark 1 and the one from the beginning of Mark 2. It is common knowledge amongst students of the Old and New Testaments that major Ancient Near Eastern narratives typically "front load" the most significant characters, characterizations, and plot devices, thus enabling the hearer the possibility of a comprehensive, informed "read" of the narrative. For a convenient presentation of each of the four Gospels, see Morna D. Hooker, *Beginnings: Keys that Open the Gospels* (Harrisburg, PA: Trinity Press International, 1997). For a detailed treatment about the union between Jesus and God in terms of Jesus' exercise of divine prerogatives found in the Old Testament, see the doctoral dissertation of Daniel Lars Magnus Johansson, "Jesus and God in the Gospel of Mark: Unity and Distinction," Ph.D. diss. (Edinburgh: The University of Edinburgh, 2012).

13. The anarthrous "Son of God" implies "the" since the narrative does not argue that Jesus is "a" (=generic) son of God.

14. See the entry under section 12.5: "Son of God," in J. P. Louw and Eugene A. Nida, *Greek-English Lexicon of the New Testament: Based on Semantic Domains*, 1st ed., 2 vols. (New York: United Bible Societies, 1988), 141.

15. For example, the term "Son of God" occurs at Mark 1:1, 11; 3:11; 9:7; 12:6 (implied); 14:61 (implied); 15:29. Each of these references disclose dimensions of "Son of God" by speech or action, hence their global qualities.

16. That is, the hidden God initiates the Son's messianic, historical mission of salvation by sending "my messenger [John the Baptist] ahead of you, who will prepare your [the Son's] way" (Mark 1:2-3 NRSV; LXX Isa 40:3 [Exod 23:20; Mal 3:1]).

17. See Collins, *Diakonia*, 73-194 for pre-Christian literary evidence that supports the essential nature of the *diakon-* word complex as "one sent," and pp. 193-244 for the New Testament and post-New Testament Christian witness to this meaning. For a review of literature up to 2005, see H. L. Chronis, "To Reveal and to Conceal: A Literary-Critical Perspective on 'the Son of Man' in Mark," *New Testament Studies* 51 (2005): 459-81.

18. The phrase "the heavens were opened" (present middle-passive participle: "being torn") is a divine passive indicating the direct action of God expressed in passive voice.

The Mystery of Jesus as Deacon

19. Morna D. Hooker, *The Gospel According to Saint Mark*, 2nd ed., Black's New Testament Commentaries (Peabody, MA: Hendrickson Publishers, 1993), 47–48. For a detailed review of possible OT and Intertestamental sources, see Robert H. Gundry, *Mark: A Commentary on His Apology for the Cross* (Grand Rapids, MI: Eerdmans, 1993), 49–53.

20. In the Pentateuch, the high priest is anointed (Exod 29:7; Lev 7:13; 8:12; see also for High Priest, Lev 4:5-7, 16; Num 35:25, etc.), they had a sacred mission, ministry cultic practices. The priest has a special relationship with God and a restricted mission, ministry in the divine cult. In our case, Jesus is identified as [the] Son of God, marking his identity as ontologically related to God, not by anointing but by nature.

21. There is no implication that Jesus becomes Son at his baptism in the text. Adoptionist theories have no support because the narrative as a whole does not signal Jesus' progressive "divinization."

22. Mark 1:14–15 is, of course, a summary, a synthesis of what Jesus no doubt proclaimed many times. The context for this synthesis is significant. Mark chose a setting with no specific geographical reference or specific hearers of the proclamation. Jesus seems to be proclaiming to "the many" (Mark 10:45), which includes any reader at any time. This statement is global. The Christocentric locus (Jesus is by himself, he speaks his own words) suggests a dramatic emphasis on the unique presence of God, God's gospel, God's kingdom in and through the historical Jesus.

23. The kenotic identity is also assumed in the "global" parables: that of the sower (Mark 4) and of the wicked land tenants (Mark 12), key "micro-plotters" for, respectively, the first and second halves of this Gospel.

24. I take this compound noun to mean "out of (*ex*) [his] own existence, being (*ousian*)."

25. Limitations in space will not permit a detailed treatment of all occurrences of the title "Son of Man." This title is a central expression of Jesus' self-understanding (Mark 2:10, 28; 8:31, 38; 9:9, 12, 31; 10:33, 45; 13:26; 14:21, 41, 62). He undoubtedly used it throughout his whole ministry, if not his whole life. On this point, see Francis J. Moloney, "Constructing Jesus and the Son of Man," *Catholic Biblical Quarterly* 74 (2013): 719–38.

26. The phrase "to be tempted" suggests a sustained, ongoing action and is best translated as "testing" (not temptations to sin, which certainly are also implied) because of its association with the desert/wilderness tradition in the OT. For a convenient presentation on these

issues, see John R. Donahue and Daniel J. Harrington, *The Gospel of Mark*, Sacra Pagina Series (Collegeville, MN: Liturgical Press, 2002), 66. Wilderness and wild beasts are associated with evil powers, see Psalm 22; Ezekiel 34. Psalm 91:11-13 connects the care of angels with safety among beasts, see Gundry, *Mark*, 66. See also Hooker, *Saint Mark*, 50-51.

27. Scholars who pursue historical, biblical, and other backgrounds to 1:13 do not agree. See Gundry, *Mark*, 60-62.

28. Is the ministry only at the end of the forty days or throughout? There is no scholarly consensus. The weight of OT references could support the proposal that angelic ministry took place throughout the "journey in the desert."

29. The two verbs "to take" and "raise her up" are in paratactic form, that is, suggesting simultaneous action.

30. As a way of pointing out the theological freight carried by the language surrounding this healing/exorcism of Peter's mother-in-law, note that in Mark, "to raise up" is associated with resurrection/resuscitation and other healings (2:9, 11, 12; 3:3; 5:41); John the Baptist's imagined resurrection (6:14, 16); exorcism (9:27); healing of a blind man (10:49); general belief in the resurrection of the dead (12:26); Jesus' Resurrection (14:28; 16:6, 14). The association of the theologically loaded *"raised"* with the mother-in-law's healing and ministry at least implies that something larger is at work other than the exorcism/healing.

31. It is commonly accepted that the verb "to follow" is a technical word for discipleship. Its application to various groups includes a ministry of service, for example, apostles (1:18; 2:14; 10:28). It describes various groups besides the apostles who indeed did follow him. For example, disciples (2:15; 6:1; 14:13); a crowd (3:7; 5:24; 11:9); crowd and disciples (11:9). Jairus follows Jesus after Jesus accepts his request to minister to his young daughter (5:24). Jesus calls anyone from the multitude to follow him and his way of the cross (8:34), but who also follow him to Jerusalem (10:32). There is the call to the rich young man (10:21), blind Bartimaeus is healed and follows (10:52); Peter follows Jesus right up to the High Priest's courtyard (14:54); the faithful women who ministered to Jesus follow him to the cross (15:41). The term used by Jesus to invite the apostles suggests a kind of imitation or participation in Jesus' life and ministry (1:17).

32. Recall that in Hebrew, Greek, and Latin, the words for *assembly*, *congregation*, and *church* are feminine.

33. I'm reading the aorists as historical present, which highlights the effect of the immediacy of Jesus' words. In addition, these aorists

are to be taken as summary occurrences (because of the indicative mood) because of their global nature, as distinguished from a simple, one time occurrence. See James A. Brooks and Carlton L. Winbery, *Syntax of New Testament Greek* (Washington, DC: University Press of America, 1979), 89.

34. The many historical challenges regarding the provenance of "Son of Man" have been well documented, see Adela Yarbro Collins, "The Origins of the Designation of Jesus as 'Son of Man,'" *Harvard Theological Review* 80, no. 4 (1987): 391–407. See notes below for work done after 1987.

35. It is a salvific, suffering servant who is *sent* by God, Collins, *Diakonia*, 42–62.

36. Chronis argues that the Son of Man both conceals the Son of God identity under the theme of "messianic secret" in order to reveal the works and words of a divine person, Mark's Son of God, cf. Chronis, "To Reveal and to Conceal," 466–76.

37. Leim proposes the following: "Jesus as the Son of Man who so participates in the activity and identity of Israel's God that he is the filial embodiment of YHWH. The eschatological revelation of YHWH in the Son of Man is not only continuous with, but grounded in, the narrative's fundamental proclamation of Jesus as Son of God." See Leim, "In the Glory of His Father," 216.

38. The irony here is great. There can only be one Son of God in the Roman Empire, namely, Caesar Augustus. It is pure irony that an imperial representative of the emperor—a centurion—proclaims another Son of God. In imperial terms, such a proclamation by an imperial agent would be the equivalent of deification but also sedition. Cf. Craig A. Evans, "Mark's Incipit and the Priene Calendar Inscription: From Jewish Gospel to Greco-Roman Gospel," *Journal of Greco-Roman Christianity and Judaism* 1 (2000): 67–81.

39. In particular, see the unresolved issues on diaconal sacramental identity in chapter 7: "Theological Approach to The Diaconate in the Wake of Vatican II," 91–110, esp. 93–97, 103–4, Commissio Theologica Internationalis, *From the Diakonia of Christ to the Diakonia of the Apostles*, North American ed. (Chicago: Hillenbrand Books, 2003).

40. On the significance of the spiritual dimension of diaconal existence, see National Conference of Catholic Bishops, Bishops' Committee on the Permanent Diaconate, 2005 no. 141n63, 111–12.

3.

Christ as Servant

WILLIAM M. WRIGHT

Each of the four canonical Gospels contain stories and sayings in which Jesus explicitly identifies himself as a servant. In Matthew and Mark, the most obvious account concerns the request from James and John (or their mother, as in Matt 20:20) for positions of honor in the kingdom of God (cf. Matt 20:20-28; Mark 10:35-45). In the course of his response, Jesus teaches that those with status in the kingdom of God must aspire to be the slaves of others—in stark contrast to the ways of Gentile kings and sovereigns. Jesus then presents himself and his redemptive death, in particular, as the mode of humble service: "For the Son of Man came not to be served but to serve, and to give his life a ransom for many" (Mark 10:45 NRSV; Matt 20:28). The parallel alignment of the two infinitival clauses "to serve" (*diakonēsai*) and "to give his life" (*dounai tēn psychēn*) presents these two actions as coinciding. Jesus' mission and his work as servant find their fullness in his redemptive death on the cross. Whereas Matthew and Mark locate this episode on Jesus' journey to Jerusalem, Luke features a comparable account within the context of the Last Supper (Luke 22:24-30). Responding to a squabble among the disciples over who was the greatest among them, Jesus again contrasts the mode of humble service proper to the kingdom of God with the ways of Gentile sovereigns (Luke 22:24-25). Again, he is the model of humble service, but with a different saying: "I am among you as the one who serves" (Luke 22:27).

Conceptually—and without any judgment about literary dependence—John's Gospel provides an interesting theological synthesis of these elements noted in the Synoptic Gospels. Similar to Luke, the Fourth Gospel provides the most extensive display of Jesus as servant at the Last Supper in the account of the washing of the feet, which, like the end of the accounts in the Gospels of Matthew and Mark, also contains a deep connection between Jesus' washing the feet of his disciples and his death on the cross. These theological convergences attest to the accuracy of Luke Johnson's observation: "What is left implicit in the synoptic Gospels is made explicit in [John]."[1]

Since it draws together the themes also found in the Synoptics, let us focus on the Fourth Gospel's presentation of Christ as Servant with special attention to the account of the washing of the feet (John 13:1-20).[2] An examination of this text, as well as other related ones in John, reveals a twofold contribution. First, it demonstrates how Christ's service—both that done by Christ and that done by others in obedience to Christ—is "cruciform."[3] In other words, such service is identified and formed by Christ's perfect gift of his life on the cross. Second, this cruciform service, which is incumbent on all disciples, remains foundational to the ministry of those given a unique share in Christ's work, as evident in the presentation of Peter in John 21. While the Fourth Gospel does not include much about sacramental orders (including the diaconate), it does provide us with substantive teaching about Christ's service and a biblical setting for our continued thinking about the diaconate.

THE CRUCIFORM SERVICE OF CHRIST (JOHN 13:1-20)

John begins the second major section of his Gospel narrative, the so-called "Book of Glory" (John 13–21), by narrating a series of events at the Last Supper (13:1-30). After some introductory, narrative commentary (13:1-3), the evangelist states that Jesus "got up from the table, took off his outer robe, and tied a towel around himself. Then he poured water into a basin and began to wash the disciples' feet and to wipe them with the towel that was tied around him" (13:4-5 NRSV). Like many other actions performed by Jesus during his public ministry, Jesus' washing the feet of his disciples at the Last Supper is a prophetic gesture,[4] whereby the prophetic actor discloses particular contents or claims through symbolic action. Through his skillful narration of this event, John invites his audience to discern several, interrelated dimensions of this symbolic act of Jesus.

The act of washing the feet of the disciples is a prophetic anticipation of Jesus' death.[5] John presents this dimension of Jesus' action in a variety of ways. First, the washing of the disciples' feet (13:1-3)—which opens the Book of Glory (John 13–20)—recalls motifs pertaining to Jesus' death already established in the Gospel. For instance, John announces that Jesus' "hour had come" (13:1),[6] and through his hour, Jesus will return to the Father who sent him (13:1, 3).[7] John also mentions Judas's impending betrayal of Jesus, which comes at the instigation of Satan, the primary opponent of Jesus in the Gospel, who will be "driven out" by Jesus' death (12:31).[8] Also significant is the statement that Jesus "having loved his own who were in the world, he loved them to the end (*eis telos*)" (13:1 NRSV). As is his common compositional technique, John employs the phrase "to the end" in multiple, interrelated senses: Jesus loves "to the end" in the sense of the maximum or upmost, and he does so by loving "to the end" of his mortal life.[9] The mention of "end" (*telos*) also recalls previous mention of Jesus' completing (*teleioun*) his Father's work (cf. 4:34; 5:36).[10] Thus, through this narrative introduction to the Book of Glory (13:1-3), John invites his audience to view the account of the washing of the feet in terms of Jesus' approaching death and his loving "to the end."

Second, the account of the washing of the feet is also a prophetic anticipation of Jesus' death through its powerful clash with cultural conventions. In particular, there is great incongruity between who Jesus is and what Jesus does. The Gospel has already established Jesus as the incarnate Word (1:14), the Son of Man who has come from the Father to reveal him and do his saving will (3:13; 6:38; 8:40), and the one who is "I AM" (6:20; 8:28, 58)—the one sharing the very identity of YHWH.[11] Moreover, within the cultural context of the ancient Mediterranean world, Jesus has a superior social status as a religious teacher and head of a band of disciples. He is their social superior, and they owe him loyalty and deference.[12] Indeed, after washing the feet of the disciples, Jesus reiterates his superior status with his words to the disciples, "You call me Teacher and Lord—and you are right, for that is what I am" (13:13 NRSV).[13]

When Jesus, who is both the incarnate Word and the disciples' "Teacher and Lord," arises during dinner and washes his disciples' feet, he does something profoundly and shockingly dissonant with cultural convention. Given that most people in antiquity traveled by foot, thus making one's feet quite dirty, it was a gesture of hospitality to offer guests water to bathe their feet.[14] Moreover, culturally speaking, feet were considered a shameful, or a lower-status, part of the human body. Thus, the actual work of washing another's feet would be reckoned as base, degrading work, and it would be performed by a person of low status, namely a slave.

By washing the feet of his disciples, Jesus, their "Teacher and Lord," humbles himself to do the work of a slave. The superior lowers himself to perform for his subordinates a service, which would be below even them to do.[15] The act of washing the feet is a profound act of total self-emptying and self-humbling for the sake of his disciples. In other words, it is kenotic and thus conceptually congruent with Paul's statement in the famous Christ-hymn in Philippians: Jesus "though he was in the form of God…emptied himself, taking the form of a slave" (Phil 2:6-7). The account of the washing of the feet is a prophetic anticipation of Jesus' death because it is a symbolic enactment of what Jesus will literally do on the cross: the incarnate Son of God descends to the lowest depths of human existence and makes a total gift of his life in loving obedience to the Father for the salvation of the world.

These aspects—the cultural incongruity and the connection to Jesus' death—are both captured in the exchange between

Peter and Jesus in 13:6-10. When Jesus goes to wash Peter's feet, the disciple, recognizing the cultural incongruity, addresses Jesus as "Lord" (*kyrie*) and asks "are you going to wash my feet?" (13:6). Jesus responds, "You do not know now what I am doing, but later you will understand" (13:7 NRSV). By contrasting Peter's present lack of comprehension with a future state of understanding, Jesus presents the action as an event with hidden meaning (a mystery), the depths of which will be taught to the disciples by the Paraclete after the resurrection (14:26; 16:13).[16] Exemplifying what Jesus has just said about his lack of understanding, Peter then issues a strongly worded, emphatic protest, "You will never wash my feet" (13:8).[17] Thinking in terms of cultural convention and the stunning breach that such an action constitutes, Peter displays an attitude of refusal and resistance toward Jesus' action for him.

But Jesus summons Peter to an attitude of receptivity, not resistance: "Unless I wash you, you have no share with me" (13:8 NRSV). Jesus does not deny the cultural incongruity of his actions (in fact, his subsequent comments in vv. 13-15 confirm it). Instead, Jesus calls upon Peter to yield and consent to his Master's self-emptying and self-humbling action for his sake. Given that Jesus has already established that the washing of the feet is an action with hidden meaning, it is not simply the case that Peter must only allow Jesus to wash him physically at the Last Supper—as his well-meaning but misguided response to Jesus suggests, "Master, then not only my feet, but my hands and head as well" (13:9). Rather, more profoundly, Peter must yield to that which the action of washing the feet prophetically anticipates—and thus participates in: Jesus' self-humbling and self-emptying gift of his life on the cross. For it is only by receiving the benefits effected by Jesus' death on the cross that Peter can "have...a share with [Jesus]" (13:8 NRSV), that is, to participate in the divine communion, to share in Jesus' own life and relationship with the Father as the Son.

A second dimension of this prophetic action, which presupposes its relation to Jesus' death, is the moral example that it sets for the disciples. After washing the disciples' feet, Jesus returns to his place at the table and reiterates his status as their superior: "You call me Teacher and Lord—and you are right, for that is what I am" (13:13 NRSV). Having affirmed his superior status, Jesus then connects it to the lowliness of his action and summons his disciples to imitate him: "So if I, your Lord and Teacher, have washed your feet, you also ought to wash one another's feet. For I have set you an example, that you also should do as I have done to you" (13:14-15 NRSV). John's Gospel refers to the action as "an example" (*hypodeigma*), a familiar term in the world of Greco-Roman moral discourse, where it was commonplace to use moral examples for imitation.[18] Jesus instructs his disciples to imitate his example of humbling, self-emptying action for the sake of others. The action of washing the disciples' feet is thus substantively the same as Jesus' love command, the other great instruction, which Jesus gives to his disciples at the Last Supper in John.

On three occasions in the Farewell Discourse (John 14–17), Jesus commands his disciples to love in imitation of his own love: "I give you a new commandment: love one another. As I have loved you, so you also should love one another" (13:34; 15:12, 17). Like the washing of the feet, Jesus' own practice serves as the model and the impetus for that of the disciples. The more substantive elaboration of the love command in 15:12-17 draws out the intrinsic relationship between Jesus' love and his death on the cross. After Jesus issues the love command for the second time in the Farewell Discourse, he elaborates on its substance: "No one has greater love than this, to lay down one's life for one's friends" (15:13). Not only does Jesus explicitly identify love with "laying down one's life," but this Greek phrasing—featuring the verb "to put, place" (*tithēmi*) along with the object "life" (*psychē*)—also picks up other instances in John's Gospel where Jesus speaks of his death on the cross in terms of laying down his life.

One is reminded, here, of the several occasions in the Good Shepherd Discourse (John 10:1-18) where Jesus speaks of laying down his life for the sheep (10:11, 15, 17-18). A key rhetorical strategy by which this discourse achieves its theological goal is the series of contrasts between the various characters, actions, and groups given in figurative language. Jesus contrasts himself as the good shepherd with the hired man on the specific matters of their respective relationships with the sheep and actions in the face of mortal danger to the flock (10:11-13). For instance, whereas the hired man "who is not a shepherd and whose sheep are not his own" (10:12), Jesus identifies himself as "the good shepherd" (10:11) who "calls his own sheep" (10:3). When confronted by the wolf—an enemy and mortal danger to the flock—the hired man abandons the sheep, leaving them to be harmed by the wolf (10:12) because he "does not care for the sheep" (10:13 NRSV). By contrast, "the good shepherd lays down his life for the sheep" (10:11 NRSV). The hired man abandons the sheep to save himself, but the good shepherd gives his own life for the sake of the sheep. As Jerome Neyrey has argued, it is the shepherd's self-sacrifice for the good of his flock that (among other things) makes the shepherd "good," or "noble" (the latter being Neyrey's preferred translation of the Greek *kalos*).[19]

The language of "laying down one's life" also appears in the closing words of this discourse. Jesus says, "For this reason the Father loves me, because I lay down my life in order to take it up again. No one takes it from me, but I lay it down of my own accord. I have power to lay it down, and I have power to take it up again. I have received this command from my Father" (10:17-18 NRSV). These words are significant because they present Jesus' death on the cross as his self-gift. Jesus chooses to go to the cross and makes a total gift of his life by "laying it down." Moreover, Jesus does this with perfect freedom—hence, his comment "no one takes it from me." Jesus freely lays down his life in obedience to the Father, and this act of obedience is simultaneously an act of love. As in the Farewell Discourse, Jesus says, "but I do as the Father has commanded me, so that the world may know that I love the Father" (14:31 NRSV). By going to the cross, Jesus makes a perfect gift of his life out of love and obedience to the Father, and he does so for the welfare of his sheep.

When Jesus commands his disciples to "love one another as I love you" (15:12), he instructs them to put into practice the same kind of total self-giving for the good of others, which he himself enacts on the cross. Just as Jesus loves by freely giving his life on the cross, out of love and obedience to the Father and for the world's salvation, so too are his disciples to practice the same kind of self-giving love in obedience to Jesus: "You are my friends if you do what I command you" (15:14). The love command, therefore, is a verbal articulation of what Jesus does symbolically in the washing of the disciples' feet and literally on the cross. The love command is substantively the same as the command to "wash one another's feet" (13:14). Whether given verbally in the love command or symbolically in the washing of feet, Jesus' self-emptying, self-giving love and obedience on the cross is the moral example for the disciples' conduct.

The cross, therefore, provides the essential shape and identity for the loving practice of Jesus' disciples. In other words, Christian love and its specific instantiation in the form of service is cruciform. Jesus' disciples are to imitate in practice the same kind of self-giving love and obedience that Jesus displays on the cross. This cross-informed love is fundamental to the whole of Christian life. Not only is the love command the major practical teaching given by Jesus in the Fourth Gospel, but he also singles it out as a marker and witness to others of Christian identity: "By this everyone will know that you are my disciples, if you have love for one another" (13:35 NRSV).

The Fourth Gospel thus teaches that cruciform love should inform and pervade all Christian conduct. This remains the case and finds unique expression in those disciples who are given a unique share in the service of Christ and his flock. To illustrate this point, let us now turn to the account of Peter's exchange with the risen Jesus at the end of the Gospel.

PETER AS DISCIPLE AND LEADER (JOHN 21:15-19)

In this well-known encounter between the risen Jesus and Peter in John 21:15-19, Peter three times professes his love for Jesus, and Jesus in turn gives Peter a share in his role as good shepherd.[20] Through his skilled narration of this scene, John weaves together a variety of theological threads involving both leadership and discipleship. Significant for our purposes are the ways in which John presents Peter here as both disciple and leader, as both sheep and shepherd. By presenting Peter in this dual role, the evangelist shows how cruciform love and service, which is incumbent on all disciples, remains essential to and finds unique expression in Peter's ministry. Through his ministry, Peter becomes conformed in both office and practice to Jesus, the Good Shepherd.

On the one hand, this episode underscores Peter's identity as a faithful disciple of Jesus. By recalling details surrounding Peter's threefold denial of Jesus (18:15-18, 25-27), this encounter between the risen Jesus and Peter comes to light as the undoing of those denials and Peter's consequent restoration as a disciple. Just as Peter had three times denied Jesus (thus completely disowning him), while keeping warm by a "charcoal fire" (18:18), so now Peter three times professes his love for Jesus before a "charcoal fire" (21:9), the one on which Jesus has been making breakfast. Peter's restoration as a disciple of Jesus rests on his threefold profession of *love* for Jesus, underscoring the fundamental place of love in Christian discipleship: "By this everyone will know that you are my disciples, if you have love for one another" (13:35 NRSV; cf. 15:12, 17).

Peter's identity as a disciple of Jesus is also attested by the twice-repeated command of Jesus to Peter: "Follow me" (21:19, 22). The Fourth Gospel often uses the verb *akolouthein* to designate being a disciple, but especially relevant for present purposes are the uses of *akolouthein* in the Good Shepherd Discourse—given the other associations between John 21:15-19 and this passage. In the Good Shepherd Discourse, Jesus says that the sheep follow him (the Shepherd) because they know his voice. They will not follow a stranger (10:4-5). Later, Jesus adds, "My sheep hear my voice. I know them, and they follow me" (10:27). By telling Peter to "follow" him, Jesus both confirms and reinforces Peter's place as a disciple with respect to Jesus.

And yet, the risen Jesus also invests Peter with a unique share in his role as the good shepherd of the sheep. After each time Peter professes his love for Jesus, Jesus in turn gives Peter a pastoral task and responsibility: "Feed my lambs" (21:15); "Tend my sheep" (21:16); "Feed my sheep" (21:17). The shepherd was a common image for leadership in Mediterranean and Near Eastern antiquity.[21] Other than Jesus, Peter is the only one in the Fourth Gospel to be assigned such pastoral tasks, giving him a leadership role as a designate (or vicarious) shepherd to the sheep.

However, there are subtle differences between Jesus as Shepherd and Peter as shepherd, such that while their roles are similar, they are not the same. For instance, none of the Greek verbs used in John 10:1-18 articulating Peter's responsibilities—"to feed" (*boskein*) or "to tend" or "to shepherd" (*poimainein*)—are predicated of Jesus, the Good Shepherd. Moreover, with each pastoral commission, Jesus reiterates that the sheep—that Peter is to lead and shepherd—are "my sheep." The sheep belong to Jesus, not Peter, and Peter, in his leadership capacity, is to serve as their caretaker and custodian in imitation of the good shepherd.

As was noted earlier, the preeminent feature of the good shepherd is that he "lays down his life for the sheep" (10:11, 15). The good shepherd makes a free, sacrificial gift of his life for the welfare of his sheep. In other words, and to use the conceptually related language of 13:1, the good shepherd loves his sheep and "loves them to the end." Thus, it is quite appropriate that this episode between the risen Jesus and Peter, wherein Jesus appoints Peter as a vicarious shepherd of his sheep, ends with discussion of Peter's upcoming martyrdom: "'when you were younger, you used to fasten your own belt and to go wherever you wished. But when you grow old, you will stretch out your hands, and someone else will fasten a belt around you and take you where you do not wish to go.' (He said this to indicate the kind of death by which he would glorify God.)" (21:18-19 NRSV).

This pairing of Peter as a disciple who "follows" along with mention of his "laying down his life" recalls his earlier exchange with Jesus at the Last Supper. After Peter asks Jesus where he will soon be going, Jesus tells him, "Where I am going, you cannot follow me now; but you will follow later" (13:36). The answer to Peter's question is, ultimately, the Father, for Jesus is returning to the Father by way of his cross and resurrection. But not grasping this, Peter protests, "Lord, why can I not follow you now? I will lay down my life for you" (13:37 NRSV), and Jesus then predicts Peter's threefold denial (13:38). These same intentions of Peter—to "follow" Jesus and to "lay down [his] life"—are revisited in John 21, when Peter is commissioned to follow Jesus even to the point where he will in fact lay down his life.

Peter's dual role as both sheep and shepherd informs the scene involving the Beloved Disciple, which immediately follows Peter's encounter with the risen Jesus. Starting from the Last Supper, the evangelist has articulated an extended comparison between Peter and the Beloved Disciple. Up until now, "Every time that Peter and the Beloved Disciple have appeared together in the Gospel…the Beloved Disciple has had a special privilege or insight that Peter did not have at first."[22] For instance, at Peter's request, the Beloved Disciple asks Jesus about the identity of his betrayer at the Last Supper, but only the Beloved Disciple learns the answer from Jesus (13:26-28). After Jesus' arrest, the Beloved Disciple gains access to Annas's courtyard and then arranges for Peter to be admitted (18:16). Whereas Peter denies Jesus three times after his arrest, the Beloved Disciple stands at the foot of the cross and receives Jesus' mother as his own (19:25-27) and then witnesses the flow of blood and water from Jesus' corpse (19:34-35). On Easter Sunday morning, the Beloved Disciple outruns Peter to the tomb (20:4), and he is the first to arrive at some insight that God's activity is the reason why Jesus' tomb was empty (20:8).[23] Moreover, in the resurrection appearance at the beginning of John 21, the Beloved Disciple is the first to realize that the risen Jesus was the one speaking to them from the beach (21:7).

However, after the risen Jesus makes him a delegate shepherd of the sheep, Peter appears in a superior place to the Beloved Disciple. The text indicates that when Peter "turned," he "saw the disciple whom Jesus loved following" (21:20 NRSV). That is, the Beloved Disciple is in a position where he is following Peter and, by implication, Jesus.[24] Peter asks about the Beloved Disciple, and after Jesus tells Peter not to worry about him, he further instructs Peter, "Follow me" (21:22). This scene thus presents Peter as both a superior leader figure as regards the other disciples, and at the same time, a subordinate and follower of Jesus. With respect to Jesus' sheep, Peter is a shepherd, but with respect to Jesus, Peter is a sheep.

In conjunction with the episode of the washing of the feet, the presentation of Peter in John 21 shows how cruciform love is foundational in the unique forms of ecclesial ministry. It is after Peter professes his love for Jesus that Jesus invests him with a unique share in his role as shepherd. Peter's love for Jesus is the foundation for his ecclesial ministry. Jesus commands Peter to "feed" and "shepherd" his flock and also to "follow" him, thus summoning Peter to obedience to Jesus as his superior. Therefore, while Peter receives a unique ministry in the service of Christ's sheep, love, obedience, and discipleship remain fundamental to this service. It is love and obedience, facilitated by the fidelity of discipleship, that conform Peter to modes of service characteristic of the good shepherd: "I will lay down my life for the sheep" (10:15) and does so out of obedience to the Father (10:18).

CONCLUSION

Therefore, in examining some major aspects of the Fourth Gospel's presentation of Christ's service—that done by Christ and by others in imitative obedience to Christ—what stands out is that such service receives its essential shape from Jesus' death on the cross. It is here that Jesus "lays down [his] life" (10:15) in perfect love and obedience to the Father and for the world's salvation. Jesus anticipates the total, self-emptying gift of his life through the symbolic act of the washing of the disciples' feet and summons them to put this kind of love into practice by giving them the love command and instructing them "to wash one another's feet" (13:14). This summons to practice self-emptying, self-giving love is incumbent on all disciples, and also finds special expression in those disciples given unique ecclesial ministries (like Peter).

All the Gospels remind us that we cannot adequately understand Christ as servant apart from Christ as crucified. More specifically, John invites us to look upon the cross in faith and see there the Son of God's free and total giving of himself for others' good, an act of self-emptying service for others. In considering the diaconate—its responsibilities, sacramental character, and relation to both the nonordained and other levels of holy orders—we should ask how this unique sacramental ministry bears a distinctive conformity to the cross of Jesus Christ. Without understanding Christ as servant apart from the cross, we arguably cannot understand the sacramental ministry of the diaconate with its demonstration of cruciform love.

NOTES

1. Luke Timothy Johnson, *Writings of the New Testament: An Interpretation*, 3rd ed. (Minneapolis: Fortress, 2010), 471.

2. The analyses that follow develop material given in Francis Martin and William M. Wright IV, *The Gospel of John* (Grand Rapids: Baker Academic, 2015), 232-38.

3. The terms *cruciform* and *cruciformity* have acquired currency in New Testament studies in significant part due to the work of Michael J. Gorman on Paul, for example, Michael J. Gorman, *Cruciformity: Paul's Narrative Spirituality of the Cross* (Grand Rapids: Eerdmans, 2001); and *Apostle of the Crucified Lord* (Grand Rapids: Eerdmans, 2004).

4. As examples of actions in Jesus' ministry (in the Gospel of John as well as the Synoptics), which would correspond to the category of prophetic gestures, one could point to the temple incident (John 2:13-22; cf. Mark 11:15-19 et par.); the calling and presence of the Twelve (John 6:67; Mark 3:13-19 and parallels); Jesus' messianic entrance into Jerusalem, enacting Zechariah 9:9 (John 12:12-16; Mark 11:1-11 and parallels). Examples of prophetic gestures from Old Testament prophets would include Jeremiah's public smashing of the potter's flask at Ben-Hinnom (Jer 19:1-15) and the many performed by Ezekiel (Ezek 4–5) to prophesy the coming conquest of Judah. This is similarly noted in Raymond E. Brown, *The Gospel According to John*, Anchor Bible 29-29A, 2 vols. (New York: Doubleday, 1966-70), 2:568.

5. See also Edwyn Clement Hoskyns, *The Fourth Gospel*, ed. Francis Noel Davey (London: Faber & Faber, 1947), 437; Brown, *John*, 2:568; Rudolf Schnackenburg, *The Gospel According to St. John*, trans. Kevin Smyth et al., 3 vols. (New York: Herder & Herder and Crossroad, 1968-82), 3:18.

6. See John 2:4; 7:30; 8:20; 12:23, 27.

7. See John 7:33; 8:21; cf. 8:14; 9:5; 12:35 (where Jesus' departure is implied). Talk of Jesus' departure will continue in John 14:4, 28; 16:5, 10, 17.

8. John firmly establishes Judas's identity as Jesus' betrayer from his first appearance in the Gospel. See John 6:70-71; 12:4. For further discussion, see William M. Wright IV, "Greco-Roman Character Typing and the Presentation of Judas in the Fourth Gospel," *Catholic Biblical Quarterly* 71 (2009): 544-59.

9. The best examples of this technique include John's use of the adverb *anōthen*, meaning "again" and "above," to speak of being born "again" and "from above" (John 3:3, 7) and his use of the verb *hypsoun* ("lift up") to speak of Jesus' being lifted up physically on the cross, which is simultaneously his being lifted high or exalted (John 3:14; 8:28; 12:32).

10. John will continue to use verbs related to *telos* to articulate Jesus' completing his Father's work by giving his life on the cross: *teleioun* (17:4, 23; 19:28) and *teloun* (19:28, 30).

11. Here I draw on the "divine identity Christology" articulated by Richard Bauckham. See his *Jesus and the God of Israel: God Crucified and Other Studies on the New Testament's Christology of Divine Identity* (Grand Rapids: Eerdmans, 2008), esp. 1-59.

12. See Wright, "Greco-Roman Character Typing," 552-53.

13. There may also be a very subtle claim to divinity here, for the Greek term in 13:13-14 is *kyrios* ("Lord").

14. See Bruce J. Malina and Richard L. Rohrbaugh, *Social-Science Commentary on the Gospel of John* (Minneapolis: Fortress Press, 1998), 219-20.

15. See Martin and Wright, *Gospel of John*, 237.

16. See Ignace de la Potterie, "The Truth in St. John," in *The Interpretation of John*, 2nd ed., ed. and trans. John Ashton (Edinburgh: T&T Clark, 1997), 78; reprinted from *Rivista biblica italiana* 11 (1963): 3-24; William M. Wright IV, "The Theology of Disclosure and Biblical Exegesis," *The Thomist* 70 (2006): 406-9.

17. The Greek phrasing of Peter's protest (*ou mē nipsēs mou tous podas eis ton aiōna*) drives home this emphasis with its two negatives (*ou* and *mē*) and the expression for "forever."

18. See Abraham J. Malherbe, *Moral Exhortation: A Greco-Roman Sourcebook* (Philadelphia: The Westminster Press, 1989 [1986]), 135–38; "[*hypodeigma*]," in *A Greek-English Lexicon of the New Testament and Other Early Christian Literature*, 2nd ed., ed. Walter Bauer, William F. Arndt, F. Wilbur Gingrich, and Frederick Danker (Chicago: University of Chicago Press, 1979), 844.

19. See Jerome H. Neyrey, "The 'Noble' Shepherd in John 10: Cultural and Rhetorical Background," *Journal of Biblical Literature* 120 (2001): 267–91, esp. 281–87.

20. This analysis depends on Martin and Wright, *Gospel of John*, 351–55.

21. See Martin and Wright, *Gospel of John*, 189.

22. Ibid., 355. The list of examples that follows appears on p. 14.

23. For argumentation, see William M. Wright IV, "Inspired Scripture as a Sacramental Vehicle of Divine Presence in the Gospel of John and *Dei Verbum*," *Nova et Vetera*, English Edition 13 (2015): 159–61.

24. Martin and Wright, *Gospel of John*, 355.

PART II
Diaconate and Tradition

4.

The Uniqueness of the Deacon

W. SHAWN McKNIGHT

The sacramental character of the diaconate has long been an issue of theological debate, and a lack of clarity among pastors and the laity about the deacon's identity and mission in the Church continues to hamper the effectiveness of the permanent diaconate. Deacons, who struggle to meet conflicting expectations of bishops, parish priests, religious, lay ecclesial ministers, and the people in the pews, often experience role conflict.[1] These expectations are based, in part, on an incorrect or incomplete understanding of who the deacon is and his mission. The unhelpful comparison of deacons with priests is one of the fundamental reasons for the present confusion, in which deacons are either defined by what they cannot do in relation to priests, or perceived as a stopgap for the lack of priests. Deacons have, however, a unique identity and role within the Church. The permanent diaconate will only come into its own and have a meaningful impact on the life and mission of the Church when everyone appreciates this unique identity and role.

CONFUSION ABOUT THE DIACONATE

St. Thomas Aquinas, along with many scholastic theologians who espoused a Pseudo-Dionysian linear hierarchy (in which the order of the ecclesiastical ministry focused upon the central action and power of consecrating the Eucharist), held that the diaconate is indeed a sacramental order, but only insofar as it is a degree of participation in the ministerial priesthood.[2] The unity of the sacrament of holy orders was, for them, rooted in the ministerial priesthood. This vision of the sacrament of holy orders supported the practice of the *cursus honorum*, whereby a candidate for the priesthood had to pass sequentially from the lower ranks before obtaining the highest, the ministerial priesthood, which entailed the supreme spiritual power to confect the Eucharist. In this schema, the subdiaconate and diaconate were thought to be degrees of participation in the ministerial priesthood of Jesus Christ sufficient for a permanent, sacramental character, whereas the "minor orders" lacked such character. Furthermore, the conferral of the office of the episcopacy was not understood to be a sacramental ordination but a consecration, wherein all the spiritual powers of the priesthood already given at the candidate's ordination to the presbyteral rank were juridically freed up for ministry. This scholastic understanding of holy orders, however, is not the teaching of the Second Vatican Council, which greatly benefited from the rich discovery of key patristic texts in the nineteenth century.

The Dogmatic Constitution on the Church, *Lumen gentium* (LG), and the Decree on the Mission Activity of the Church, *Ad gentes*, present a theology of the diaconate that reclaims an understanding of the sacrament of holy orders without its reduction to the ministerial priesthood. Language such as "strengthened through the imposition of hands," "bound more closely to the altar," and "through the sacramental grace of the diaconate" conveyed the Council Fathers' certain teaching that ordination to the diaconate entails a sacramental character that configures the *ordinandus* to Christ and thereby confers sacramental graces for his ministry.³ In distinction to the Scholastics, however, they also taught that deacons are ordained "*non ad sacerdotium, sed ad ministerium.*"⁴ This phrase, which has its origins in the third-century text known as the *Apostolic Tradition of Hippolytus*, is the theological basis upon which theologians must develop organically the unique sacramental identity of the deacon. The nuance between "*sacerdotium*" and "*ministerium*" needs to be made more clearly, for hidden within these words lie the distinctions between the deacon and the presbyter. As previously noted, the Scholastics held that the deacon participates (in a lesser degree) in the ministerial priesthood of Christ. The *sacerdotium* was, for them, the very definition of the sacrament of holy orders. Insofar as an order participated in the *sacerdotium*, it entailed a configuration to Christ in accord with the spiritual powers (*ad posse* for the priest, *ad licere* for the deacon) given with reference to the Eucharist; hence, the diaconate had a sacramental character because it participated in a limited degree in the *sacerdotium*.⁵

One must acknowledge that a small number of theologians today still adhere to the scholastic notion of the diaconate, and unfortunately, the limitations here prevent a complete rebuttal of such theological positions. Here, we intend to present a developed theological understanding of the diaconate that is organically related to the teaching of the Council. One might simply refer, however, to the *Catechism of the Catholic Church* (*Catechism*) promulgated by St. John Paul II, and the Apostolic Letter *Omnium in mentem* of Pope Benedict XVI for the revision of the Code of Canon Law (CIC), to respond to those who either deny the sacramental character of the diaconate or who still insist upon relating it essentially to the ministerial priesthood.

Interestingly, both the original text of the CIC of 1983 and the draft edition of the *Catechism* (originally composed in French) presented an incorrect understanding of the diaconate precisely because they espoused the scholastic vision of the deacon. In Canons 1008 and 1009 of the original text, a theological description of the entire ecclesiastical order was given using language that could certainly be applied to the bishop, and secondarily to the priest, but not to the deacon:

> Can. 1008: By divine institution some among the Christian faithful are constituted sacred ministers through the sacrament of orders by means of the indelible character with which they are marked; accordingly they are consecrated and deputed to shepherd the people of God, each in accord with his own grade of orders, by fulfilling in the person of Christ the Head the functions of teaching, sanctifying and governing.
> Can. 1009: §1. The orders are the episcopacy, the presbyterate, and the diaconate.

Taken together, Canons 1008 and 1009 §1 explicitly connect the diaconate with the role of "fulfilling in the person of Christ the Head the functions of teaching, sanctifying and governing," language singularly associated with the ministerial priesthood.

This theological mistake has been corrected in the revision promulgated by Pope Benedict XVI. Canon 1008 now reads, "By divine institution, some of the Christian faithful are marked with an indelible character and constituted as sacred ministers by the sacrament of holy orders. They are thus consecrated and deputed so that, each according to his own grade, they may serve the people of God by a new and specific title."[6] And the revised canon 1009 now includes an additional paragraph, which reads, "Those who are constituted in the order of the episcopate or the presbyterate receive the mission and capacity to act in the person of Christ the Head, whereas deacons are empowered to serve the people of God in the ministries of the liturgy, the word and charity." These combined revisions tether the CIC more closely to the official magisterial teaching of the Council on the diaconate found in LG 29. At once affirming the sacramental character of the diaconate, they also appropriately distinguish what the deacon and his service are not: neither priestly nor presidential.

Regarding the *Catechism*, it is worth noting that a deliberate effort was also taken on the part of its editors to correct inconsistent language involving the ordained ministry in the provisional edition. For example, the original French version and English first edition of the *Catechism* of 1994 made the following unsophisticated statement on the sacrament of holy orders:

> No one can bestow grace on himself; it must be given and offered. This fact presupposes ministers of grace, authorized and empowered by Christ. From him, they receive the mission and faculty ("the sacred power") to act *in persona Christi Capitis*. The ministry in which Christ's emissaries do and give by God's grace what they cannot do and give by their own powers, is called a "sacrament" by the Church's tradition. Indeed, the ministry of the Church is conferred by a special sacrament. (no. 875)

This text, as it stood, was inconsistent with the teaching of LG 29, since no distinction was made concerning the deacon and his particular configuration to Christ in comparison to that of the priestly orders. Curiously, at number 1554, the English first edition of the *Catechism* was precise about the distinction of the diaconate from the episcopacy and presbyterate.[7]

The second English edition of the *Catechism* of 1997–a translation of the official Latin *editio typical*–revised paragraph 875 in the following manner:

> From him, bishops and priests receive the mission and faculty ("the sacred power") to act *in persona Christi Capitis*; deacons receive the strength to serve the people of God in the *diaconia* of the liturgy, word and charity, in communion with the bishop and his presbyterate.

The editors of the *Catechism* recognized the inaccuracy of the previous text and took extra care to distinguish the deacon from the other clergy, carefully avoiding language of *tria munera* (the threefold office of Priest, Prophet, and King) and *in persona Christi Capitis* for the diaconate. This specific change in the text brought the typical edition of the *Catechism* into conformity with the teaching of LG 29 on the deacon.

Yet, one may continue to ask the following: To what does the unity of the sacrament of holy orders adhere, if not the ministerial priesthood? And what is so unique about the ministry of the diaconate in distinction to the other two orders?

THE UNITY OF MISSION IN THE SACRAMENT OF HOLY ORDERS

In order to understand the uniqueness of the diaconate, it is necessary first to explore what all three orders have in common and why we have only one sacrament of holy orders. While the Magisterium certainly teaches that the deacon is not a priestly order, what is not so clear, however, is the meaning of the phrase "*diaconia* of liturgy, word and charity" used by the Council fathers to describe the ministry of deacons in relation to the ministry of priests and bishops, who alone have a share in the threefold office of Christ the Priest, Prophet, and King through the sacrament of holy orders. In using this phrase, the Council fathers did convey that there is a diaconal way to participate in the ecclesiastical ministry. However, an unsophisticated interpretation of the biblical word *diakonia* might lead one to think that it refers only to the diaconate, when in fact it represents for the Council an understanding of ministry that applies to all three orders and connotes the character of service. For example, in LG 24, the Fathers used *diakonia* to describe the office of the bishop: "This office which the Lord entrusted to the shepherds of his people is a true service, and in holy scripture it is significantly called 'diaconia' or ministry."[8] *Diakonia* is not a word implying something specifically diaconal, but rather the common element among the three orders in their specific relationships to Christ. One could say that the Second Vatican Council replaced the *sacerdotium* of the Scholastics with the biblical (and patristic) concept of *diakonia* as the underlying and unifying reality of the one sacrament of holy orders.

The revolutionary word study by John Neal Collins rejects the notion that *diakonia* in the bible concerns the ambit of menial tasks or the notion of humble service, which by custom have long been associated with the diaconate. In fact, he asserts that the *diakon-* word group actually signifies the fulfillment of a noble charge or mandate.⁹ With this paradigmatic shift in meaning, we can now make sense of the various uses of the title "deacon" in the New Testament, such as when "*diakonos*" is ascribed to Christ, Paul, the apostles, ordinary disciples, and those who served more formally within the Church in close proximity to the *episcopoi*. Collins's consideration of Acts 6 is also rather fascinating in light of his word study. He advocates interpreting the role of the seven as a new group of preachers who conveyed to the widows of the community the daily message preached by the apostles in the temple area, not a daily distribution of food. Rather than connoting the menial service of a waiter at table, the mission of a "deacon" signified by *diakonia* would relate more to the work of a herald, emissary, messenger, or ambassador at court, functions that are more readily understood as pertaining to the ministry of the apostles themselves. Deacons, Collins asserts, fulfilled the charge of someone over them within the Church and served as a go-between or intermediary between individuals or between groups. Thus, it would have been entirely appropriate for the New Testament writers to employ the *diakon-* word group when describing the individuals who worked closely with the *episcopoi* in fulfillment of the apostolic ministry.¹⁰

This biblical notion of *diakonia* and its association with the diaconate are echoed in the third century *Apostolic Tradition of Hippolytus* (AT). The AT, as previously mentioned, is the original source (by way of the later *Egyptian Church Order*) for the theological teaching of LG 29 that the deacon is ordained "*non ad sacerdotium, sed ad ministerium*."¹¹ The original text in the AT, however, is worded a bit differently from what appears in *Lumen gentium*. In the section concerning the ordination of a deacon (AT 8), there is an instruction with an explanation of diaconal ordination, as well as the ordination prayer itself. In the explanatory section, we read,

> In the ordination of a deacon, the bishop alone shall lay on hands, because he is not being ordained to the priesthood, but to the service of the bishop, [*non*

in sacerdotio ordinatur, sed in ministerio episcopi] to do what is ordered by him [*ut faciat ea quae ab ipso iubentur*]. For he does not share in the counsel of the clergy, but administers and informs the bishop of what is fitting; he does not receive the common spirit of seniority in which the presbyters share, but that which is entrusted to him under the bishop's authority. For this reason the bishop alone shall ordain a deacon; but on a presbyter the presbyters alone shall lay hands, because of the common and like spirit of their order.[12]

The deacon is ordained "*in ministerio episcopi, ut faciat ea quae ab ipso iubentur.*" What is meant by the words "*in ministerio episcopi*"? The word *episcopi* could be understood in the objective sense—that the deacon is ordained to minister to the bishop—or in the subjective sense—that he is ordained to the bishop's ministry. With the former, the object of the deacon's ministry is the bishop himself. With the latter, the community of the Church is the object of the bishop's ministry, and therefore, the object of the deacon's ministry. The phrase "*ut faciat ea quae ab ipso iubentur*" might lead one to believe that ministry or service to the bishop is intended, since the deacon is "to do what is ordered by" the bishop. If this be the case, then how should we take into account the ordination prayer in the AT that states, "Give the holy Spirit…to this your servant whom you have chosen *to serve your Church*"? Furthermore, AT 34 gives an example of what is meant by service to the bishop and service to the Church: "Each deacon, with the subdeacons, shall attend on the bishop. They shall inform him of those who are ill, so that, if he pleases, he may visit them. For a sick man is greatly comforted when the high-priest remembers him." The deacon is ordained to the ministry of the bishop in the subjective sense; that is, the deacon's direct ministry to the Church is under, and in the context of, the presiding ministry of the bishop. In this manner, the unity of the one ecclesiastical ministry is maintained while recognizing the deacon's distinct participation in that ministry.[13]

The main import of the phrase is to clarify that though the

deacon shares in the bishop's ministry, the deacon's ministry lacks sacerdotal quality. This ministry of the deacon does not, however, make him merely a personal servant of the bishop. Deacons are not in the personal service of the bishop, but are ordained for the ministry for which the bishop is responsible. And that ministry held by the bishop has the community as its object. LG 20 reaffirms this notion of ordained ministry when it states, "The bishops, therefore, have undertaken along with their fellow-workers, the priests and deacons, the service of the community." In what sense, therefore, do we interpret the phrase "*ut faciat ea quae ab ipso iubentur*"? Since the bishop is primarily responsible for the ecclesial ministry in its totality, he alone, as high priest and president of the assembly, has the responsibility of distributing the work of the Church among its members according to their specific charisms. Consequently, the deacon must do that which is ordered by the bishop. There is no contradiction between the deacon attending the bishop as head of the local *ekklesia* and the deacon's service to the Church at large. In this manner, the deacon's particular ministry to the people of God is nestled within the unity of the one ecclesiastical ministry.

    The deacon receives the gift of the Spirit and a share in the one charge given to Christ by the Father, and then by Christ to the apostles, and now by the Spirit to the bishop. He works with the bishop, under his presidency, to build up the Church in a particular place, for the praise and glory of God. It is, therefore, not unreasonable to say that, according to the AT, the deacon has a share in the bishop's apostolic office, which has as an objective to safeguard and promote the apostolic identity of the local church. It is the divine charge of the bishop to keep watch over the apostolicity of the church so that the Church is always recognized as a gift of God.[14]

    Since the deacon is ordained "to the bishop's ministry," diaconal ministry draws directly from the episcopal ministry. In our desire to investigate the unique ministry of deacons in the Church today, it behooves us to consider the ministry of the bishop as articulated by the Council.[15] In LG 18–27, the Council sets forth its most authoritative teaching on the office of the episcopacy. The decree on the pastoral office of bishops in the Church, *Christus dominus* (CD), considers the pastoral implications of the teaching in LG, but adds nothing to the doctrinal understanding of the bishop's ministry. We shall therefore follow the dogmatic teaching as presented in LG, integrating pertinent concrete examples articulated in CD as appropriate.

The gist of the Council's teaching found in LG about the bishop rests in three central themes: the sacramental nature of the episcopacy (art. 21);[16] the intrinsic connection of the various *munera* of the bishop (art. 21); and the function and dignity of the college of bishops (art. 22ff.). In LG 18-20, the Council explores the significance of the Catholic teaching that the college of bishops has taken the place of the college of apostles as pastors of the Church by divine institution. The language of "sacred power" is used to describe the transmission of authority and grace that comes by way of the apostolic succession through the imposition of hands (LG 21). The "fullness of the sacrament of order," called the "supreme priesthood,"[17] is received through the episcopal consecration that confers the offices of teaching, governing, and sanctifying. In an eminent and visible way, bishops take on the functions of Christ and act in his person. This sacred ministry is entrusted to the bishops, in whom the apostolic tradition is "manifested and safeguarded" (LG 20). With priests and deacons as their helpers, bishops receive the charge of the community, "presiding in the place of God over the flock, whose shepherds they are, as teachers of doctrine, priests of sacred worship and ministers of government."

Every bishop, as a member of the college of bishops, has responsibilities to the universal Church as well as to the local church in which he is "the visible principle and foundation of unity" (LG 23). Our concern lies primarily in the ministry of the bishop as it pertains to the local church, in which deacons assist him. The description of the bishop's ministry in the local church is structured along the lines of the *tria munera*.[18] In articles 24 and 25, the *munus docendi* is described as "among the principal tasks of bishops." Bishops are "heralds of the faith," "teachers endowed with the authority of Christ." They are to make the faith bear fruit in the lives of the faithful and "vigilantly ward off errors that are threatening their flock" (LG 25). Reminiscent of the AT, CD 12 states the bishops' duty to show the faithful "the way divinely revealed for giving glory to God." A way of praising God is pointed out in the preaching of social justice. Bishops are to "take particular care to further the interests of the poor and the underprivileged to whom the Lord has sent them to preach the gospel" (CD 13). Already, we note possibilities for the ministry of the deacon in assisting the bishop's ministry by encouraging the practice of biblical justice among the members of the local church.

Through the sacred ministry of the bishop, the people of God are sanctified (LG 26). The celebration of the Eucharist is entrusted to the bishop's oversight, "by which the church continuously lives and grows." The sacramental life of the local church is directed by the bishop, "to whom has been entrusted the duty of presenting the worship of the Christian religion to the divine majesty, and of regulating it according to the commands of the Lord." Thus, bishops are to exhort and instruct their people "so that in the liturgy, especially in the holy sacrifice of the mass, they fulfil their part with faith and devotion." "Deacons likewise have been ordained for the ministry," states CD 15, implying that they are to assist the bishop "as promoters and guardians of the whole liturgical life in the church which has been entrusted to them." It is their endeavor to make "the faithful acquire a deeper knowledge of the paschal mystery, and so live through the Eucharist that they may form one closely-knit body united in the love of Christ." Under his *munus sanctificandi*, the bishop serves the holiness of the local assembly entrusted to his care. The function of the deacon within as well as beyond the liturgy could assist the people, who have dispositions of a suitable heart and mind, to take a full, conscious, and active part in liturgical celebration.[19]

By counsel, persuasion, example, authority, and sacred power, the bishop governs the local church (LG 27). The pastoral authority of the bishop is not to be used for his personal gain but is in service to the Gospel. Bishops are to remember "that the greater must become as the younger and the leader as one who serves." Bishops have the right and duty "of directing everything that concerns the ordering of worship and the apostolate." Serving not as vicar of the Pope but as president of the people he governs, the bishop is not to "refuse to listen to his subjects whom he looks after…and whom he exhorts cheerfully to cooperate with him." In exercising their pastoral function, bishops should be in their flock as "good shepherds who know their own sheep and whose sheep know them" (CD 16). They are to form their whole flock "into one family, conscious of their own duties," to live and work together "in a union of charity" (CD 16).

Significantly, the Council Fathers were concerned that bishops be solicitous for the welfare of their flock:

> They must be better prepared to give guidance for the welfare of the faithful according to the circumstances of each. Accordingly they must strive to acquire an accurate knowledge of their needs in the social conditions in which they live, using for this purpose the appropriate methods, especially those of social research. They must show themselves to be concerned for all no matter what their age, condition or nationality; no matter whether they are natives, immigrants or visitors. In exercising this pastoral care they must respect the place proper to their faithful in the affairs of the church, acknowledging also their duty and right to work actively for the building up of the mystical body of Christ.[20]

In this passage, the Council has taken special care to point out the necessity of the bishop to be in tune with what is happening in the lives of his people. The deacon could assist the bishop in this task without taking on roles of a priestly or presidential nature. The necessity of the bishop to acquire knowledge of the needs and social conditions of his people provides an expansive field in which the charisms of the diaconate could be put to use.

Under the *munus regendi*, therefore, the bishop is to use his authority to form the flock entrusted to him in ever greater communion. Through the exercise of the episcopal charisms, members of the local assembly are brought to life and encouraged to take a more active role in worship and in the life and mission of the Church. The pastoral authority of the bishop functions not to control the dispensation of charisms to the faithful—for they come from baptism and not through his office—but to bring them to life so that they may be exercised in harmony in fulfilling the mission of the Church. As the concrete point of unity, it is under the charge of the bishop that the activities of the Church are ultimately coordinated. As president of the eucharistic assembly, it is the duty of the bishop to divide the work of the Church among the people of God according to charisms received in baptism and ordination.

The overall duty of the bishop is to promote unity among the people of God by safeguarding and promoting the fundamental gospel principles in the life of the Church. The bishop works to preserve the apostolic identity of the local church through his tasks of teaching the true faith, promoting right worship, and encouraging the practice of justice and charity. It is his responsibility to help all members make their own contribution, according to their various charisms. As the sovereign high priest, the bishop functions as the center of unity and inspiration of the faithful. In the language of Ephesians, he is "to equip the saints." In the language of the AT, he is to help the local church praise and glorify God.

In order to build up the Body of Christ, everyone is to fulfill his or her particular role in bringing the gospel to life in the world. It is worth noting the connection between the Church and her mission, between ecclesial *koinonia* and engagement of the world. "If there is no Church of God without its being missionary, there is no missionary Church unless it is welded into the unity of the Body of Christ."[21] There cannot be one without the other. Thus, the bishop's task in safeguarding the apostolic faith, worship, and life also involves safeguarding and promoting *koinonia* so that the mission of the Church (*diakonia*) might be accomplished. Baptism and Eucharist, as the fundamental sacraments of unity, are also therefore the fundamental sacraments upon which the charisms of the ordained ministries stand. The work of the one ecclesiastical order is to promote an authentic baptismal and eucharistic life among the people of God, nothing more and nothing less. The bishop's ministry is truly a *diakonia*, where christological, pneumatological, and ecclesial principles are at play.

The fundamental charge of Christ to all those in holy orders is the service (*diakonia*) of the communion of the Church. Bishops, priests, and deacons all share in the responsibility to preserve the apostolic character of the flock entrusted to them; namely, fidelity to the teaching of the apostles, solidarity with the poor and the practice of gospel virtues, and unity in Christian liturgy. All these characteristics constitute—sometimes more and sometimes less—the apostolic character of any Christian community.

Taken at the level of the individual, a Christian is one who—again, more or less—professes the one true Faith, who lives in conformity to the teachings of Christ, and who prays as Christ has taught us. The Rite of Christian Initiation of Adults concerns the immersion of catechumens and candidates into this threefold dimension of Christian existence. Initiation into the Church necessarily entails an intellectual conversion, a moral conversion, and a ritual conversion, all without exception. One cannot truly be a Christian in the full sense with only one or two of these marks. All three are intimately bound up with one another, as reflected in the old adage *lex orandi, lex credendi*, with the appropriate addition of *lex vivendi*. As we unlock the mysteries of the Christian faith with our minds, so we enter more deeply into the very celebration of these mysteries. Conversely, more profound experiences of the celebration of the mysteries teach and manifest tangibly to our senses what we believe. In like manner, the mutual relationship between liturgy and life, as well as ecclesial life and faith, are readily understood.

In a general sense, all three dimensions of Christian existence are necessary for salvation and they are what constitute the apostolic character of a community of believers. Communion with the Church of the apostles is both diachronic and synchronic: it has to do with preserving our relationship with the Church throughout the centuries, as well as our communion with each other in the present. The bishop and his presbyterate fulfill their charge to preserve the communion of the Church by their service as priest-shepherds, although at different levels. The bishop has responsibility for the universal Church as a member of the College of Bishops, and has particular responsibility for a local church as head of the presbyterate. The priest has responsibility for the local church as a member of the local presbyterate, which often includes particular responsibilities for a parish. In these ways, bishops and presbyters are both spoken of as "priests," though they are not of the same degree.

Deacons are also vested with a charge to preserve the communion of the Church but without the power to act *in persona Christi Capitis*. Even though the deacon does not share in the ministerial priesthood, it is understandable that the Magisterium would speak of his service in terms of *diakonia* in the three areas of liturgy, word, and charity because these three areas have to do with the communion of the Church. Yet, the area of emphasis for the deacon is not so much *diakonia* of liturgy or even *diakonia* of the Word, though these should always be recognized as part of his ministry. Ministerial service of the Word and ministerial service in the liturgy do not present unlimited opportunities for deacons to acquire new roles that are uniquely their own because of the limits of Sacred Tradition. The greatest opportunity for the deacon to flourish in his ministry of preserving the communion of the Church is in the realm of ecclesial life and mission. The deacon can provide a distinct service from his own unique place in the network of relationships that is the Church.

Neither a priest-shepherd nor simply another member of the flock, the deacon is uniquely positioned to serve the communion of the church by serving the bond of communion between the flock and its shepherd, and by reinforcing and vivifying the solidarity that exists between the Christian community and those in need. Surely, bishops and priests bear responsibility for their own relationships with their people. But the tradition of the Church, particularly that seen in the church orders of the Patristic era, reveals the deacon as a crucial ligament in the relationship between the shepherd and the members of his flock. Regarding charitable works and the practice of social justice, it is sensible for the Church to dedicate the order of deacon to the work of animating the Christian faithful in the fulfillment of this important aspect of the Church's mission. In fact, these two principal functions of the deacon in the Church's life and mission (i.e., facilitating the relationship between bishops/priests and the rest of the faithful, and being a driving force for the service of charity) provide sufficient grounds for the distinctive ministry of the deacon flowing from his unique sacramental configuration to Christ the Servant. What, then, are the duties of the deacon that are not priestly or presidential functions? What unique service does (or could) the deacon render to the local assembly under the auspices of the bishop?

THE UNIQUENESS OF THE DEACON

Following the closure of the Second Vatican Council, Pope Paul VI issued several documents concerning the implementation of the permanent diaconate as outlined by the Council.[22] The final document, the Apostolic Letter *Ad pascendum*, prophetically articulated the role of the deacon more fully than the conciliar texts:

> Finally, Vatican Council II approved the wishes and requests that, where it would lead to the good of souls, the permanent Diaconate should be restored as an intermediate order (*medius ordo*) between the higher grades of the ecclesiastical hierarchy and the rest of the people of God, being as it were a mediator (*interpres*) of the needs and desires of the Christian communities, an animator of the service or *diaconia* of the Church among the local Christian communities, and a sign or sacrament of Christ the Lord himself, who *came not to be served, but to serve*.[23]

Paul VI identified the deacon as an intermediary between the higher grades of the Church's hierarchy and the rest of the people of God. While one could interpret "intermediate order" as an intermediate stage in a linear hierarchy, it is more likely here to have a different meaning. In the context of the ecclesiology of the Second Vatican Council, Paul VI's understanding of the intermediary nature of the deacon's order more than likely connotes *mediation*, bringing together more closely two entities, rather than *separation*. The deacon would not be a barrier, or buffer zone, between the higher clergy and the laity, but instead, he would function more like a bridge or glue, binding everyone together more closely. This understanding is apparent in the following phrases, where the deacon's ministry is rooted in the needs of the people, as an animator of the Church's *diakonia* as a whole, and as a symbol of Christ the Servant. Fulfilling these tasks, the deacon brings about a greater communion among the people of God, rather than serving as an additional rank-figure in the structure of power and authority between the bishop and priests on the one hand, and the laity on the other.

Paul VI's description of the diaconate as an "intermediate order" between the sacerdotal orders and the Christian faithful provides a theological grounding for the diaconate's uniqueness. According to the *New Webster's Dictionary* an "intermediate" is "someone through whom two other parties communicate."[24] The presence of an intermediate subject makes real dialogue possible between parties who are not in direct communication with one another. The concept of the diaconate as an intermediate order leads us to consider its service in terms of support for dialogue among the people of God. Dialogical structures ensure the proper distribution of knowledge of and responsibility for the life and mission of the Church among all her members. Such ministry would ultimately promote greater communion, for the unity of the local church depends upon fruitful dialogue between her members. If indeed the deacon were a part of the dialogical structure of the Church, then this reality would be theologically significant in our search for a more fundamental *raison d'être* of the deacon.

Theologically, the deacon is *other* than the bishop and his priests, and he is *other* than the laity. While distinctly *other*, the deacon is nonetheless directly related to both the clergy of a higher grade (by virtue of ordination) and the laity (by virtue of not sharing in the presidency of the assembly). The deacon therefore stands not only in the unique position as *other*, but is also *among* the people of God. From this dual perspective, the nature of the diaconate allows the deacon to serve as an intermediary, whether in the specific dialogue between shepherd and flock, or generally among the people of God as a whole.

In the *National Directory for the Formation, Ministry and Life of Permanent Deacons in the United States*, the United States' bishops flesh out the vision of Pope Paul VI by articulating special tasks for those in the diaconal order.[25] Here, the bishops describe a particular way the deacon is to promote the participation of the laity in the life and mission of the Church: "The deacon has a special role to promote communion and to counter the strong emphasis on individualism present within the United States" (no. 57). And the bishops continue, "In his preaching and teaching, the deacon articulates the needs and hopes of the people he has experienced, thereby animating, motivating, and facilitating a commitment among the lay faithful to an evangelical service of the world" (no. 58). While neither of these functions are uniquely diaconal (for bishops and priests share in these tasks), deacons have open to them a unique way to fulfill them.

When discussing the deacon's role in the practical aspects of charity, the bishops recognize the uniqueness of the deacon:

> Although all those in sacred orders have a responsibility to preach justice, the deacon may have a particular advantage in bringing this message to the laity because he lives and works in the secular world. The deacon, because of his familiarity with the day-to-day realities and rhythms of the family, neighborhood and workplace, can relate the rich tradition of Catholic social teaching to the practical problems experienced by people. He also may serve to link the Catholic Church to other Christian communities, other faith traditions, and civic organizations to

address pressing social needs and to foster a collaborative sharing of material resources and personnel in response to those needs.[26]

What the bishops of the United States articulate in these passages is not so much a list of particular tasks for the deacons to perform (such as what is found in LG 29), but rather areas of responsibility that pertain to the apostolic ministry and that can be accomplished in an unlimited number of ways. Furthermore, deacons are uniquely positioned to fulfill these apostolic responsibilities in a way that is not possible for celibate priests and bishops.

Deacons have been given the general assignment from the bishops to assist them and the priests to overcome a particular spiritual malady for the Church in the United States, what one might call American individualism. This would require an effective employment of the entire ministry of the diaconate in word, sacrament, and charity, as the poisonous effects of individualism have seeped into the mindset and behavior of Catholic Americans, even at times affecting the celebration of the liturgy. By helping bishops and priests to become more aware of the needs and desires of the Christian faithful, especially those on the margins (a particular emphasis of the pontificate of Pope Francis), and by animating the laity to fulfill their responsibilities with those who are in need, the deacon serves the apostolic communion of the Church like no one else can. The diaconate can be structured so as to forge the bond of communion between the shepherd and his flock, and to foster the link between the Catholic faithful and those on the margins—even beyond the Church. But the role of the deacon should not compete with or in any way impede the participation of anyone in the life and mission of the Church. The image of the master of ceremonies in the liturgy serves as a good analogy of what the ministry of the deacon should look like in the Church.

The *Ceremonial of Bishops* states, "The master of ceremonies wears either an alb or cassock and surplice. Within a celebration a master of ceremonies who is an ordained deacon may wear a dalmatic and the other diaconal vestments."[27] It is significant that when a priest serves as a master of ceremonies, as is often the case, he does not vest according to his order. This is because the function of a master of ceremonies in the liturgy is not presbyteral. When a deacon performs this role in the liturgy, however, he is exercising a liturgical function that matches his sacramental character. It is entirely appropriate that he fully vest as a deacon when assuming this role. To be sure, people are chosen to serve as a master of ceremonies because they have a particular competence to perform the role. All things being equal, however, a deacon is the most theologically apt person in the community of the Church to perform this role since his ministry outside the walls of the church is consumed with helping others to fulfill their own.

Within the Mass, a good master of ceremonies is as transparent as possible, for his sole purpose is to facilitate the flow of the liturgy without drawing attention to himself. He prepares, anticipates, directs, encourages, and helps the entire assembly to fulfill their functions with grace. He is the designated worrier for the assembly, which relies upon him when the unexpected occurs. The reason we have masters of ceremony is that the presence of a bishop, priests, other ministers, and the full assembly demand it. The master of ceremonies does not replace or substitute for anyone. This is an important clarification of the role of the deacon in the Church vis-à-vis priests and the laity. It is often heard that the reason for the restoration of the diaconate is a lack of priests. One could not be further from the truth. Although the local bishop may rightfully tap members of the diaconate to fulfill extraordinary needs presented by a dearth of priests, we should not reduce the diaconate to this extraordinary situation. The Church needs the ministry of deacons today not solely because of the absence of priests, but more importantly, *because* we have priests and bishops! The understanding of the deacon as a unique minister of communion, as reflected in the role of the deacon master of ceremonies, reveals that the ministry of the deacon does not replace or substitute for the ministry of priests but enhances and enriches the fulfillment of their apostolic obligations.

As we recognize that there are numerous possibilities for the deacon's ministry in the Church today, we must keep in mind that the uniqueness of the deacon pertains to his identity and not just his way of fulfilling specific roles. Whether deacons serve in prison ministry, hospital chaplaincy, or in ministries to diverse cultural groups and immigrants, whether they have assignments that are parochial or diocesan-wide, the deacon is always and everywhere a symbol of Christ the Servant.

Through the sacrament of holy orders, the deacon is configured to Christ in order to fulfill the mandate of all those who are in the ecclesiastical ministry: he is to preserve the apostolic communion of the Church. But the deacon's configuration is different from that of those in the priestly orders. Because of their unique relationship to Christ, deacons are spiritually empowered to continue the mission of Christ who came to fulfill the will of his Father in heaven, even to the point of death on the cross. With priests and bishops, deacons carry out the ministry of Word, sacrament, and charity, but only the deacon is preserved from the responsibility and baggage of shepherding Christ's flock. From their distinctive position within the Church, and with their unique diaconal voice, deacons serve as a constant reminder to us all that our own participation in the life and mission and the Church is not about us. Through the sacrament of holy orders, the deacon is uniquely marked or wounded to share in Christ's self-emptying, who took on the form of a slave. The sacramental character of the deacon does not provide him with a position of governance in the Church, like that of the bishop and priest, but instead, gives him the capacity and freedom to serve, as needed, everyone else in their participation in the life and mission of the Church—even bishops and priests. In this manner, deacons are unique ministers of the Church's communion.

NOTES

1. Frank R. DeRego and James D. Davidson, "Catholic Deacons: A Lesson in Role Conflict and Ambiguity," in M. Cousineau, ed., *Religion in a Changing World. Comparative Studies in Sociology* (Westport, CT: Praeger, 1998), 94.

2. St. Thomas Aquinas provides the most extensive theological treatment of the deacon in the medieval period. His writings exerted

enormous influence on the theology of the diaconate until the Second Vatican Council. See his *Summa Theologiae Tertiam Partem*, q. 64, art. 1; q. 67, art. 1; q. 71, art. 4; q. 82, art. 3; *Supplementum Tertiae Partis*, q. 35, art. 2; q. 37, art. 2, art. 4, art. 5; q. 40, art. 7.

3. Second Vatican Council, *Ad gentes*, no. 16. The English translation of all conciliar decrees are taken from Norman Tanner, ed., *Decrees of the Ecumenical Councils: Volume II* (Trent-Vatican II), (Washington, DC: Georgetown University Press, 1990).

4. Second Vatican Council, *Lumen gentium*, no. 29.

5. Herbert Vorgrimler, "The Hierarchical Structure of the Church, with Special Reference to the Episcopate, Article 29," in H. Vorgrimler, ed., *Commentary of the Documents of Vatican II*, Volume I [*Das Zweite Vatikanische Konzil, Dokumente und Kommentare*, translated by L. Adoplphus, K. Smyth, and R. Strachan] (New York: Crossroad, 1967-89), 226-30.

6. Pope Benedict XVI, Apostolic Letter "Motu Proprio" *Omnium in Mentem* (October 26, 2009).

7. *Catechism* (1994), no. 1554: "Catholic doctrine, expressed in the liturgy, the Magisterium, and the constant practice of the Church, recognizes that there are two degrees of ministerial participation in the priesthood of Christ: the episcopacy and the presbyterate. The diaconate is intended to help and serve them. For this reason the term *sacerdos* in current usage denotes bishops and priests but not deacons."

8. Tanner, *Decrees*, 2:868.

9. John N. Collins, *Diakonia: Re-interpreting the Ancient Sources* (New York: Oxford University Press, 1990).

10. See especially John N. Collins, *Deacons and the Church: Making Connections between Old and New* (Harrisburg, PA : Gracewing/Morehouse Publishing, 2002), 47-58.

11. The Council officially cites *The Egyptian Church Order*, an early liturgical treatise that, as a result of the research of R. H. Connolly, *The So-called Egyptian Church Order and Derived Documents*, Texts and Studies 8.4 (Cambridge: 1916), and E. Schwartz, *Über die Pseudoapostolischen Kirchenordnungen* (Strasbourg: 1910), is now commonly identified as dependent upon the *Apostolic Tradition of St. Hippolytus*.

12. *Apostolic Tradition*, no. 8; translation from Geoffrey Cuming, *Hippolytus: A Text for Students*, Liturgical Study 8 (Bramcote: Grove Books Limited, 1976), 13.

13. Alphonse Borras and Bernard Pottier, *La grâce du diaconat*.

Questions actuelles autour du diaconat latin (Bruxelles: Cerf, 1998), 25-26.

14. Ibid., 26-28.

15. Obviously, an exhaustive study of the bishop's ministry cannot be done within the parameters of this essay. For an extensive bibliography, see Christopher O'Donnell, "Bishops," in *Ecclesia: A Theological Encyclopedia of the Church* (Collegeville, MN: Liturgical Press, 1996), 56-57.

16. It is noted that the Council only "teaches" the doctrine of the sacramental nature of the episcopacy without proposing a solemn definition.

17. Bernard Cooke gives five different definitions for the term *priesthood* used by the Council, sometimes without discrimination, in "'Fullness of Orders': Theological Reflections," *Jurist* 41 (1981): 153.

18. The doctrine of the three offices of Christ was only developed fully in Catholic theology in the nineteenth century, particularly by canonist, along the lines suggested by Protestant models. See, for example, Johann Franzelin, *Theses de Ecclesia Christi* (Rome: Typographia Polyglotta, 1887), esp. 43-64. This way of describing the episcopal ministry is problematic, to say the least, in that the same model is used to articulate the role of the laity in the life and mission of the Church. For a recent and succinct presentation of this issue, see Richard Gaillardetz, "Shifting Meanings in the Lay-Clergy Distinction," *Irish Theological Quarterly* 64 (1999): 115-39.

19. See Second Vatican Council, *Sacrosanctum concilium*, nos. 11 and 14.

20. Second Vatican Council, *Christus dominus*, no. 16; Tanner, *Decrees*, 927.

21. Jean-Marie Tillard, *Chiesa di Chiese. L'ecclesiologia di communion* (Brescia: Queriniana, 1989), 39.

22. The Apostolic Letter *Sacrum diaconatus ordinem*, *Acta Apostolica Sedis* (AAS) 59 (1967): 697-704, implemented the recommendations of the Second Vatican Council by determining general norms governing the restoration of the permanent diaconate in the Latin Church; the Apostolic Constitution *Pontificalis Romani recognitio*, AAS 60 (1968): 369-73, approved the new rite of conferring the episcopacy, presbyterate, and diaconate; the Apostolic Letter *Ministeria quaedam*, AAS 64 (1972): 529-34, suppressed the minor orders and declared that entry into the clerical state is joined with the diaconate—lectors and acolytes are no longer "ordained" but "installed"; and finally, the Apostolic Letter *Ad pascendum*, AAS 64 (1972): 534-40, which clarified the conditions for admission and ordination of candidates.

23. My translation. AAS 64 (1972): 536, "Concilium denique Vaticanum II optatis et precibus suffragatum est, ut Diaconatus permanens, ubi id animarum bono conduceret, instauraretur veluti medius ordo inter superiores ecclesiasticae hierarchiae gradus et reliquum populum Dei, quasi interpres necessitatum ac votorum christianarum communitatum, instimulator famulatus seu *diaconiae* Ecclesiae apud locales christianas communitates, signum vel sacramentum ipsius Christi Domini, qui *non venit ministrari, sed ministrare*."

24. *New Webster's Dictionary and Thesaurus of the English Language*, Main dictionary section ©1972 Librairie Larousse as *The Larousse Illustrated International Encyclopedia and Dictionary*, rev. and updated 1993 (Danbury, CT: Lexicon Publications 1993), 504.

25. United States Conference of Catholic Bishops, *National Directory for the Formation, Ministry and Life of Permanent Deacons in the United States* (Washington, DC: USCCB, 2005).

26. *National Directory*, no. 149, p. 66.

27. Pope John Paul II, *Ceremonial of Bishops* (Prepared by the International Commission on English in the Liturgy, Collegeville, MN: Liturgical Press, 1989), no. 36, p. 26.

5.

Rahner in Retrospect

FREDERICK CHRISTIAN BAUERSCHMIDT

On the eve of the Second Vatican Council, Karl Rahner wrote a lengthy article on the restoration of the permanent diaconate.[1] This article outlines the thoughts of one significant theologian just prior to the Church restoring the diaconate as a distinct and permanent office: what he thought the opportunities and barriers were and how he sought to overcome those barriers.[2] Moreover, Rahner's fundamental approach, which argues for sacramental ordination to the diaconate as a permanent office as a way of sacramentalizing diaconal functions that are already being "anonymously" exercised by laypeople in the Church, remains influential. There are, however, certain problems with this approach that, with some insights from the philosopher Saul Kripke, we might address by giving priority to the sacramental naming of deacons over any particular description of diaconal function.

RAHNER'S FUNDAMENTAL APPROACH

Rahner begins with an inquiry into the very legitimacy of raising the question of the diaconate as a permanent office or ministry (in German, *Amt*) in the Church, rather than simply a transitional step on the way to the priesthood. Rahner and other advocates for restoring the diaconate had to contend with the view that the demise of the diaconate as a permanent office, rather than being a withering away or diminishment of one of the three orders of ordained ministry, was a legitimate development within the Church's ministry. For this latter position, as Rahner characterizes it, the then-current practice of the Church "is not merely one among many possibles but is also the best possible one, since it has been formed by the experience of many centuries and since its untroubled acceptance over many centuries has been considered something self-evident by the Church."[3] In other words, the restoration of the permanent diaconate was regarded by some people as an unnecessary exercise in antiquarianism and contrary to the developed practice of the Church—perhaps something analogous to restoring the ancient "order of penitents" associated with public, canonical penance.[4] If the Church abandoned the diaconate as anything more than a testing ground for future priests, presumably she had good reason for doing so; thus, the burden lay with those arguing for the restoration of the diaconate.

Rahner then clarifies certain presuppositions guiding his inquiry into the legitimacy of raising this question of the diaconate: that the diaconate is part of the sacramental *ordo* that Christ has willed for the Church; that, despite variations in its function and exercise at different times and places, the office of deacon has been conferred by sacramental ordination; that while the diaconate *can* serve as a step on the way to priestly ordination, there is nothing about the nature of the diaconate per se that makes it a "proving ground" for the priesthood.[5] With these presuppositions in place, Rahner then argues that raising the question of the permanent diaconate is legitimate because, even in his own day, the practice of the Latin Church is not the universal one, since Eastern Rite Catholics in union with Rome have preserved the diaconate as a permanent office. Furthermore, various other established sacramental practices have been changed in the past. So Rahner concludes his initial argument, claiming that "at best the present-day practice (i.e., of a purely transitional diaconate) can be put forward only with extreme caution and many reservations when one is arguing about the best and most recommendable practice and legislation for the Church of today."[6]

Having established the legitimacy of his inquiry, Rahner then explores how the different offices within the Church's *ordo* are related to each other, noting that while the threefold character of holy orders cannot be traced to an explicit institution by Christ, it can still be considered a matter of *jus divinum* because Christ has entrusted to the Church the capacity to "distribute" within the one sacrament of holy orders the various *potestates ordinis* in varying degrees to different offices. In other words, it is within the Church's power to confer upon some men (i.e., deacons) a power of office that is more restricted in scope than what is conferred on others (i.e., priests and bishops). Yet Rahner is careful to maintain that one cannot say that such a distribution *must* happen in a threefold way, or that the *potestates ordinis* must be transmitted sacramentally. Just as the bishop's power to confirm can be delegated to a priest nonsacramentally (i.e., through an administrative procedure), so too the powers of the diaconate might be transmitted to someone in a nonsacramental fashion. Indeed, Rahner notes, "It will hardly be possible to point to any function of the diaconate which the Church could not in any way bestow by an extra-sacramental authorization."[7]

While this might at first seem to argue *against* the need for a permanent sacramental diaconate—since people do not need to be ordained in order to fulfill various diaconal functions—Rahner, in a key theological move, cleverly turns matters on their head by arguing that because diaconal functions might be carried out apart from sacramental ordination, theologians ought to "have a look around the Church to see whether this office does not already actually exist and is not already exercised there as an office distinct from the priesthood."[8] In other words, are there in the Church "anonymous deacons" who exercise diaconal ministry, even though they do so in a way more restricted than sacramentally ordained deacons—specifically, in that they cannot confer solemn baptism or distribute communion?[9] Though posed initially here as a question, the notion of an "unthematic" diaconate (borrowing a term Rahner uses elsewhere in his theology),[10] already present by God's grace and ecclesial mandate in the Church, provides Rahner with his wedge for what follows.

As Rahner turns to the actual question of the opportuneness of restoring a diaconate that is both sacramentally transmitted and not a mere passage to the priesthood, he notes,

> We must always remember the distinction and right relationship between the office and the sacramental transmission of this office. These are not identical entities, nor are they—as we have seen above—absolutely inseparable entities, at least in the case of the diaconate. They are mutually related realities in the sense that the sacramental rite of the transmission of the office receives its ultimate justification from the office and not vice versa.[11]

In other words, we have sacramental transmission of offices for the sake of having offices; we do not have offices in order to sacramentally transmit them. So the question of the opportuneness of a sacramentally transmitted diaconate is really the question of the opportuneness of the office of deacon, and this office can be considered apart from its sacramental transmission. Thus, Rahner says, "We proceed from the fact that the office [of deacon] actually exists to a sufficiently large extent in the Church…and thus shows itself to be meaningful, useful and indeed necessary."[12] Where does this diaconal office exist? Not exclusively among those ordained to the diaconate (who quickly depart it for the priesthood), but in those who carry out a variety of diaconal functions, such as the duties of "proclaiming God's word, of fulfilling important administrative functions as auxiliary organs of the bishop, of teaching Christian doctrine to the rising generation, duties of catechesis of adults, marriage instruction, even—in exceptional cases—of looking after a parish which is without a priest, duties of directing Christian organizations and clubs."[13] These functions, and not simply the liturgical functions of baptizing and giving communion, constitute diaconal office, particularly in those cases where they are exercised "by an explicit commission received from the hierarchy, under the immediate direction of the hierarchy and as a direct assistance to the task of the hierarchy, as a permanent and enduring function—even in those cases where this office has not been transmitted by sacramental ordination."[14]

Therefore, the question for Rahner becomes not whether the office of deacon should be restored, since he believes it is already present in the Church, "even though only anonymously and without any exact canonical delimitation,"[15] but rather whether that office ought to be conferred sacramentally. Rahner states his argument with uncharacteristic clarity and brevity:

> (1) the office [of deacon] already exists, (2) sacramental transmission of this office is possible and (3) such a transmission, at least where the office exists, must be regarded basically and from the outset, if not as something necessary yet as something fitting and opportune.[16]

Regarding the last point, Rahner argues that while the grace of office does not *have to* be conferred sacramentally (after all, the office of the papacy is not so conferred), it is of the nature of the Church—indeed, of the incarnation—that such grace "always presses…toward some concrete tangible form and sign."[17] We should therefore have a presumption in favor of the sacramental transmission of the grace of office, but not because such grace could not otherwise be bestowed, since even the grace of baptism can be given without baptism in water (perhaps we could speak not simply of an "anonymous diaconate" but also of a "diaconate of desire"). Rather, because someone who receives the office of deacon through sacramental transmission "will accept this office and grace of office in a much more radically existential manner, on account of the solemnity, uniqueness, and indestructible effects of such a sacramental transmission of office, than if he were given more or less the same office in a different way."[18] Rahner notes quite sensibly that those who are actually fulfilling diaconal functions as a permanent vocation need the sacramental grace of office far more than those who are simply passing through on their way to the priesthood.[19]

Having established his basic theological argument, Rahner proceeds to other questions. He discusses celibacy for deacons, arguing for the appropriateness of a married diaconate, particularly given the relatively greater immersion of deacons in worldly affairs.[20] He explores at greater length the meaning of "grace of office," including how a sacramentally ordained deacon differs from a priest as well as from a layperson fulfilling the same functions, and argues that the deacon's ordination should be understood "as the divine (sacramentally tangible) promise of the help of grace which, by reason of this promise, God is ready to give in the course of the life of the office-bearer, and which he will give to the extent in which the office-bearer opens his soul more and more to this grace by trying to do justice to his office with the help of divine grace."[21] He also addresses the question of whether the diaconate should be a full- or part-time ministry, noting that there are no part-time vocations, but that one can, like St. Paul, have "a real vocation in the theological and existential sense" even when it is carried out on a part-time basis.[22] In this way, the deacon is different from the layperson who engages in apostolic work as something like a pious sideline, as commendable as that might be. He concludes with a discussion of certain practical questions, ranging from the role of national bishop's conferences in the decision to restore the diaconate in their area, to the canonical changes needed, to the financial support of deacons, to their training and whether they would need to receive "minor orders" first.

There are certain aspects of Rahner's thought that indicate a time and setting quite different from our situation over fifty years later. For example, on reflection, we might be struck by what could seem an excessive concern about the legitimacy of even raising the question of a permanent diaconate. It is a good reminder that however much misunderstanding and opposition deacons might face in certain quarters, it is now the case—at least in Europe and North America—that the burden of proof has shifted to those who *oppose* the permanent diaconate. Furthermore, it is striking how much of what Rahner says is couched in the categories of scholastic theology, both the understanding of ordination in terms of the conferral of "powers" and the "grace of office," as well as the view that a deacon should be conceived of as a somehow more "restricted" possession of the sacrament of holy orders than a priest. While Rahner is certainly not *wrong* to couch his arguments in this way (and reading the arguments can have a salutary shock value to those not used to reading scholastic arguments), we tend not to use these terms and concepts.

Nevertheless, at its heart, Rahner's argument for the permanent diaconate conceives of the relationship between "office" (or, we might say, "ministry") and ordination in a way that has become quite common in the postconciliar Church. Indeed, in some quarters, the fundamental presuppositions of his argument have become the dominant way of thinking about the economy of salvation as a whole and about the sacraments in particular. And that is this: God's grace is always already present in the world, though in a prethematic way, due to our orientation toward God as the horizon of being, an orientation that Rahner calls the *Vorgiff auf esse* (preapprehension of being). The role of Christ, and by extension the Church, and by further extension the sacraments, is to "thematize" that grace—to make explicit what is already implicit. Here, instead of employing scholastic categories of causality, Rahner substitutes epistemological categories of consciousness—or, rather, he interprets causality in terms of consciousness. To say that sacramental actions "cause" grace is to say that they make explicit what is always already implicit: God's gracious self-communication to humanity. And this sacramental pattern continues the dynamic of the incarnation, in which God's implicit self-communication to humanity attains an unsurpassable explication in Christ. This explicit self-communication of God differs, we might say, in degree but not in kind from God's implicit self-communication.[23]

This dynamic of what is unthematized being thematized—what is implicit becoming explicit—is clearly at work in Rahner's thinking about the diaconate. Just as Rahner argues elsewhere for there being anonymous Christians, who have responded in love to the real but unthematized self-communication of God,[24] so too there is an unthematized or implicit or "anonymous" or unnamed diaconate already being exercised in the Church, which could become explicit, could be "named" as such, through sacramental ordination. Such sacramental "naming" of the diaconal office, "can make the faithful more aware of the significance of the office itself, and can increase the attraction, propagation and appreciation of the office itself for and among the faithful."[25] Rahner seems not to want to say that this is *all* that ordination does, but since he believes that diaconal identity can exist implicitly prior to ordination (and even with a certain degree of explicitness, if one is working for the Church in an official capacity), and that the specific "powers" of the diaconate, including the power to baptize solemnly and distribute communion, can be granted by the Church extrasacramentally, it is difficult to see what else diaconal ordination could be doing.

The Practical Consequences of Rahner's Approach

This is not simply a theoretical issue, but it has some practical consequences. Many a deacon has been asked, "What can you do that a layperson cannot do?" and has faced the challenge of explaining what he brings to the table of a parish's ministry that is not already going on. Explaining how one can do baptisms and witness weddings just doesn't capture what it is that one has to contribute as an ordained minister. Rahner's own view that the deacon's actions, unlike the actions of the layperson, are actions of the hierarchy, while undoubtedly true, does not help much in explaining how a deacon is different from a lay ecclesial minister, or why every person exercising diaconal functions ought not be ordained (or even what counts as "diaconal functions").[26]

The notion of an anonymous diaconate operative in the Church also appears in the screening of candidates for the diaconate, where there is often an implicit or explicit presumption that the deacon's call is verified by the candidate *already* being engaged in diaconal functions, whether liturgical (serving as a lector or extraordinary minister of the Eucharist), kerygmatic (teaching children's religious education or leading a Bible study), or apostolic (visiting the sick or volunteering at a soup kitchen). We don't expect those called to the presbyterate to provide similar evidence that they are already engaging in priestly activities (unless one believes that only those who play-celebrated Mass as a child have a vocation). Yet, in the case of deacons, the idea of their ordination as an affirmation of a function they are already fulfilling appears to be operative.

But what if Rahner's way of conceptualizing the issue is misconceived? What if thinking about diaconal ordination as making explicit an office that is already being exercised apart from ordination will always leave us with puzzling questions on the scope and character of that office, as well as how the sacramental diaconate differs from the anonymous diaconate? To put the matter slightly differently, Rahner's language of "anonymous"—that is "nameless"—deacons invites reflection on exactly what is going on in "naming," as a prelude to thinking about ordination as a sacrament that "names" a ministry within the Church's *ordo*. To aid in this task, we turn to the philosopher Saul Kripke.

ANOTHER PERSPECTIVE

For Kripke, both proper names (Cicero, Nixon, Napoleon) and at least some common names (gold, tiger, heat, light) are matters not of connotation but of denotation. In other words, Kripke rejects the notion that names are compact descriptions, as it were shorthand for particular bundles of properties. Rather, names are bestowed upon things, whether individual things in the case of proper names or classes or kinds of things in the case of common names, in what he calls an "initial baptism," which fixes the reference of the term. In the case of a proper name, this bestowing may be done by means of ostension—I point at someone and say, "He is named Napoleon"—or by description—I say, "Napoleon is the person who was the Emperor of France in the early nineteenth century and was defeated at Waterloo." In the case of common names, the initial baptism might also be by way of a kind of ostension—"gold is the substance instantiated by the group of items over there"—or by description—"gold is a yellow metal."[27] In either case, however, once the initial "baptism" has taken place, the name becomes a "rigid designator" that applies to the same object or category of objects in every possible world in which that object exists.[28] In every possible world in which Napoleon exists—including ours in which he was defeated at Waterloo and a hypothetical world in which he was defeated at Paris, as well as one in which he died as a young soldier and never became Emperor of France—it is necessarily the case that *Napoleon* refers to the same individual, otherwise we could not produce a counterfactual denial that he was, for example, the Emperor of France.[29]

For subsequent members of the community of speakers, this name is "passed from link to link," on the condition that each subsequent speaker in the chain intends to refer to what the prior speaker referred to.[30] This intention suffices to secure reference even if the subsequent speaker is unaware of or mistaken about elements of the initial description (e.g., not knowing that Napoleon was defeated at Waterloo or thinking he was finally defeated at Paris). Moreover, even if it should turn out that the description that was involved in initially fixing the reference proves to be less than complete, either because some features of the description prove to be inaccurate or because it does not sufficiently distinguish the thing named from other things, the reference of the term remains rigidly fixed.

For example, let's say that within a community of speakers, the name *gold* is given to a yellow metal. Suppose Kripke says that we subsequently discover that, due to an optical illusion caused by some odd feature of the atmosphere, gold has only *appeared* to be yellow and is in fact blue (meaning, I presume, that it reflects light on the part of the spectrum that we call "blue"). Does this mean, Kripke asks, that gold has ceased to exist because our description no longer applies to anything? However, clearly the category of objects that we have been calling "gold" has not ceased to exist; it is simply that we have been mistaken about one of its properties. Likewise, it might be the case that there are objects that fit the description "yellow metal" but which are not in fact gold—for example, iron pyrite. But if the common name *gold* were simply a shorthand way of saying "yellow metal," on what basis would we say that iron pyrite is not gold?[31]

A term such as *gold*, Kripke says, "does *not* mark out a 'cluster concept' in which most, but perhaps not all, of the properties used to identify the kind must be satisfied. On the contrary, possession of most of these properties need not be a condition for membership in the kind, nor need it be a sufficient condition."[32] A term like *gold*, he says, is simply *"that kind of thing*, where the kind can be identified by paradigmatic instances. It is not something picked out by any qualitative dictionary definition."[33] It may turn out that we can come up with an identifying characteristic of gold that uniquely and exhaustively identifies it—such as being an element with the atomic number 79—but this is not required before we can apply the name *gold* as a rigid designator. The link between the name and the referent depends not upon a link between the name and a determinate set of properties, though there may well be such a link, but upon the initial bestowal of the name and its subsequent handing on within a linguistic community.

Sacramental Ordination and Naming

How might Kripke's account help us in thinking about sacramental ordination to the diaconate and address some of the issues that Rahner's account of the diaconate has bequeathed to us?[34] Kripke's account of naming would make the notion of "anonymous deacons" problematic, because such a notion seems to say that the name *deacon* is connotative rather than denotative, that it is a compressed description of a set of functions or a "cluster concept." When Rahner writes that "the sacramental rite of the transmission of the office receives its ultimate justification from the office and not vice versa," he seems to say that the naming of the sacramental office is really a compressed description of the office. But if Kripke is correct about naming, then the diaconate is not picked out by any qualitative dictionary definition based on diaconal functions, but by the bestowal of the name *deacon*—that is, by ordination—and by the historical chain by which that referent is handed on.

The question of what ordination does is answered in this Kripkean approach by saying quite simply that ordination makes someone a deacon. One becomes a deacon not by fulfilling a set of criteria that describes the diaconal office, but by being named as such by one who intends for the name to refer in the way past users had used the name. Just as when we newly identify a particular item as "gold" we are not committing ourselves to any particular description of the essence of gold (which is not the same things as denying that gold has an essence), so too ordaining a man as a deacon is not a claim that he already fulfills the description "deacon." Even were we to discover that some of the functions of the diaconal office that we had thought were constitutive of that office were *not* constitutive after all, this would not affect the bestowal of the name.[35] Understanding naming as "causal," in the way Kripke does, allows us to understand ordination to the diaconate as bestowing an identity rather than making explicit an identity that was already implicitly present in the functions already being exercised. This would seem to accord with the idea that diaconal ordination has more to do with identity or "being" rather than function or "doing." Or in other words, contra Rahner, diaconal doing (office/ministry/*Amt*) flows from the diaconal being that is sacramentally bestowed and not vice versa.

Both Rahner and Kripke are thinkers who operate at a high level of abstraction—who, as it were, describe the world from the height of ten thousand feet. But, what difference does this make at a lower altitude, from a position closer to the ground? Earlier, we noted that Rahner's theology had influenced our understanding of the diaconate in the direction of thinking that diaconal ordination was a kind of ratification of an office already present nonsacramentally, and that we consequently expected candidates for the diaconate to prove themselves by fitting into a particular description that connotatively defined the category "deacon." In some ways, this is just good sense. If we are going to ordain someone to the office of deacon, we ought to look for some evidence that he is capable and willing of doing the things we expect deacons to do. But what Kripke suggests is that we do not need a complete and exhaustive account of what a deacon is in order to impose that name on someone through the sacrament of holy orders; indeed, there is an ongoing discovery possible with regard to the adequacy of our description of the diaconate. And this discovery will come about as a result of continuing scrutiny of how ordained deacons actually exercise their ministries, just as our understanding of gold will only be enhanced through examining actual pieces of gold.

For those charged with forming deacons, this means at least two fundamental things. First, they should avoid trying to fit candidates for the diaconate into too rigid a mold of what a deacon is supposed to be. Without abandoning all exercise of prudent discernment, they should be open to the possibility that a candidate who does not quite fit the mold might actually teach them something new about what a deacon is. Second, the ongoing discernment of diaconal identity will require an ongoing engagement with those already ordained to the diaconate on the part of formators, and perhaps a more significant role of deacons in the formation of future deacons. Because it is those that have received through ordination the name *deacon* who can best show us who and what a deacon is.

NOTES

1. Karl Rahner, "The Theology of the Restoration of the Diaconate," in *Theological Investigations*, vol. 5, trans. Karl-H Kruger (New York: Crossroad, 1983), 268–314.

2. For some of the work by other theologians that forms the backdrop of Rahner's reflections on the diaconate, see the essays collected in *Foundations for the Renewal of the Diaconate*, trans. David Bourke et al. (Washington, DC: National Conference of Catholic Bishops, 1993).

3. Rahner, "Theology of the Restoration," 268–69.

4. Of course, the order of penitents may yet have its day; see, Thomas Michelet, "Synode sur la famille: la voie de l'ordo paenitentium," *Nova et Vetera* 90, no. 1 (2015).

5. Rahner, "Theology of the Restoration," 269-72.
6. Ibid., 273.
7. Ibid., 277.
8. Ibid.
9. Ibid., 277-78.
10. For example, "This unthematic and ever-present experience, this knowledge of God which we always have even when we are thinking of and concerned with anything but God, is the permanent ground from out of which the thematic knowledge emerges which we have in explicit religious activity and in philosophical reflection." Karl Rahner, *Foundations of the Christian Faith*, trans. William V. Dych (New York: Seabury Press, 1978), 53.
11. Rahner, "Theology of the Restoration," 281.
12. Ibid., 282.
13. Ibid.
14. Ibid., 284.
15. Ibid.
16. Ibid., 286.
17. Ibid., 288.
18. Ibid., 288-89.
19. Ibid., 290.
20. Ibid., 296-97.
21. Ibid., 304.
22. Ibid., 306.
23. See Rahner, *Foundations of the Christian Faith*, 170-75. I say this with some hesitation, since sometimes Rahner speaks as if God's explicit self-communication in Christ (and the Church and sacraments) is a difference in kind and not just in degree from God's implicit self-communication. But whatever Rahner himself says, the "Rahnerianism" that has trickled down from his thought makes it a difference of degree and not kind. See, for example, the remarks of Thomas O'Meara, *Theology of Ministry* (Mahwah, NJ: Paulist Press, 1999), 163.
24. See, *inter alia*, Karl Rahner, "Anonymous Christians," in *Theological Investigation*, vol 6, trans. Karl-H and Boniface Kruger (Baltimore: Helicon Press, 1969), 390-98.
25. Rahner, "Theology of the Restoration," 285.
26. For a recent attempt to answer this question, see Richard R. Gaillardetz, "Toward a Contemporary Theology of the Diaconate," *Worship* 79 (September 2005), 419-38.
27. Saul A. Kripke, *Naming and Necessity* (Cambridge, MA: Harvard University Press, 1980), 135.

28. Ibid., 48.

29. Thus, in order to meaningfully say that there is a possible world in which Napoleon was not Emperor of France, the name *Napoleon* would have to refer to the same individual both in our world and in the possible world in which he is not Emperor. See ibid., 62, where Kripke uses the example of Aristotle rather than Napoleon.

30. Ibid., 96. Kripke notes, "If I hear the name 'Napoleon' and decide it would be a nice name for my pet aardvark, I do not satisfy this condition."

31. Ibid., 118-19.

32. Ibid., 121.

33. Ibid., 122.

34. As Kripke develops his causal theory of reference, it applies to proper names as well as *some* common names—that is, those related to "natural kinds" (*Naming and Necessity*, 134). In using his account to think about sacramental ordination, however, we need to ask how applicable it would be to a nonnatural kind, since presumably the name *deacon* does not refer to a natural kind (deacons not being commonly found "in the wild," as it were). Stephen Schwartz holds that Kripke's view of names as "rigid designators" is only coherent when applied to natural kinds (Stephen P. Schwarz, "Introduction," in *Naming, Necessity, and Natural Kinds*, ed. S. Schwarz [Ithaca: Cornell University Press, 1977], 13-41, esp. 37-41). David Braun, on the other hand, has argued that Kripke's causal account of naming applies to natural and nonnatural kinds equally (David Braun, "Names and Natural Kind Terms," in *Oxford Handbook of Philosophy of Language*, ed. Ernest Lepore and Barry Smith [Oxford: Oxford University Press, 2006], 490-515). This latter view seems to be correct, since while nonnatural kinds might not have the sort of "essence" that a natural kind does, part of the force of Kripke's argument is that names as rigid designators do not depend upon our knowledge of the essence of things, but rather upon the act of bestowing the name (i.e., "baptizing") and upon the intention of subsequent users of the name to refer to what the initial bestower referred to.

35. Rahner himself backed away somewhat from the idea of "anonymous deacons" in a postconciliar essay on the diaconate, though I am not convinced that he abandoned the fundamental dynamic of the unthematized office being sacramentally thematized. See "On the Diaconate," in *Theological Investigations*, vol. 12, trans. David Bourke (New York: Seabury Press, 1974), 61-80, esp. 69.

PART III

Diaconate and Prayer

6.

The *Lex Orandi* of the Ordination Rite

DAVID W. FAGERBERG

The buzzword in this title, which requires an initial word of explanation, is the term *lex orandi*. Of the several false interpretations given, we should be careful to avoid the one that mistakenly places liturgy and doctrine in opposition to each other, for this has led some people to suppose that we can change the people's *credendi* by changing the people's *orandi*. In other words, advancing a certain ideological goal can be achieved by altering the people's prayer patterns. This mistaken approach is big on *orandi* and not so big on *lex*, whereas, on the contrary, the first word is as important as the second. The phrase *lex orandi* invites docility from us insofar as it grounds our theology in the activity of the Church, instead of grounding our theology in our own understanding. Liturgy, as Aidan Kavanagh noted, is where we find the faith of the Church in motion, and not some individual's faith. When we attempt to put the primary theology of the rite of diaconal ordination into second-order language, we should not treat this rite as a quarry from which to excavate bricks for our own theological house. We must do *lex orandi* with the support of the whole tradition behind us. We can look to liturgy for theology because here the Church is being herself, but remember that it is her mind that we want to know, not our own. We meet a person through his statements, gestures, behavior, symbolic actions, and so on, but finally it is the person we want to encounter, not the tools he uses to express himself. Similarly, liturgical studies examine the words and symbolic actions of the rite of ordination, but finally it is the mind of the Church that we want to encounter.

With this idea in mind, there is an interesting exchange at the very beginning of the ordination rite. A deacon calls the candidates forward ("Let those to be ordained deacons come forward") and then calls their names individually for each to reply, "Present." Each candidate goes to the bishop and makes a sign of reverence.

> *When the candidates are in their places before the Bishop, the Priest designated by the Bishop says:* "Most Reverend Father, holy Mother Church asks you to ordain these men, our brothers, to the responsibility of the Diaconate." (198)

Who has brought this assembly together and instigated this ordination? Who requests the life of this man for ministry? Who asks the bishop to act in his capacity as chief shepherd of his diocese and expand the hierarchy by one more man? Holy Mother Church does. In his *Apostolic Letter on Norms for the Diaconate*, Pope Paul VI says that Christ instituted a variety of ministries in the Church for the nurture and constant increase of the people of God, and then he quotes St. Ignatius of Antioch when the Church Father says, "The Deacons too, who are ministers of the mysteries of Jesus Christ, should please all in every way, for they are not servers of food and drink, but ministers of the Church of God."[1] What do Deacons serve? Not food and drink, but mysteries. Whose mysteries? Not ours, but the mysteries of Jesus Christ. Deacons are made ministers of the Church of God.

The Church served by the deacon is a complex thing, meaning composed of more than one part. *Lumen gentium* says we must understand the Church by analogy to the mystery of the incarnate Word, and this by no weak analogy. "The society structured with hierarchical organs and the Mystical

Body of Christ, are not to be considered as two realities, nor are the visible assembly and the spiritual community, nor the earthly Church and the Church enriched with heavenly things; rather they form one complex reality which coalesces from a divine and a human element" (LG 8). The Church is complex for being both visible and invisible, for having both divine and human elements. The Church is Christ's mystical body, and "this Church constituted and organized in the world as a society, subsists in the Catholic Church" (LG 8). *Lumen gentium* is only affirming the teaching of Pope Pius XII in his encyclical *Mystici Corporus Christi* of twenty years earlier. He saw twin errors about the Church, and instructed us to avoid them both. On the one side, there is a false rationalism united to a naturalism that only sees the Church as a juridical and social union; on the other side, there is a spiritualism that thinks of the Church as something hidden and invisible. The one fails to see the Church as a *mystical* body, while the other fails to see the Church as a mystical *body*. So he writes, "We think, how grievously they err who arbitrarily claim that the Church is something hidden and invisible, as they also do who look upon her as a mere human institution possessing a certain disciplinary code and external ritual, but lacking power to communicate supernatural life" (*Mystici Corporus Christi* 64). Now, when the bishop asks the candidate if he is resolved "to be consecrated for the Church's ministry," it is both of these dimensions that the deacon will serve. The deacon will be as mistaken if he thinks he is serving something hidden and invisible, as if he thinks he is serving a merely human institution. If he were only serving a human institution, then we might adequately describe the diaconate by a review of the functions he performs. But if the deacon, in fact, becomes a minister of both the mysteries and the body in which they subsist, we must consider not only what he does but what he becomes in the sacrament of ordination. This is not an equivocation; it is not an ambiguity or ambivalence; it is an antinomy. Deacons serve both the visible assembly and the spiritual community, the earthly Church and the Church enriched with heavenly things.

THE SACRAMENT OF ORDINATION

The identity of a deacon is sacramental. Therefore, it is appropriate to examine the sacrament of ordination that creates the deacon. Now, the sacrament happens within a liturgical rite—as do they all—and the meaning of the sacramental act is conditioned by its liturgical matrix. If we were to adopt a minimalist approach, we would only need to consider matter and form, which is easily found in the 1968 Apostolic Constitution for the Rites of Ordination. There, Paul VI aligns himself with the 1947 Apostolic Constitution by Pius XII named *Sacramentum ordinis*, in which is declared, "The sole matter of the sacred orders of diaconate and presbyterate is the laying on of hands; likewise the sole form is the words determining the application of this matter…." Since Paul VI considers the purpose of the 1968 revision to restore texts to the form they had in antiquity, to clarify expressions, and to emphasize the effects of the sacrament, he promises to "declare what are to be held as the essentials [of matter and form] in each revised rite." Concerning the matter, he repeats that it is the laying on of hands; concerning the form, he says it "consists in the words of a consecratory prayer, of which the following belong to the essence and are consequently required for validity." And what follows in the Constitution are the words of form for each of the three degrees of ordination. Here they are for the case of a deacon:

> Lord,
> send forth upon them the Holy Spirit,
> that they may be strengthened
> by the gift of your sevenfold grace
> to carry out faithfully the work of the ministry.[2]

The current translation of the rite renders them this way:

> Send forth upon them, Lord, we pray,
> the Holy Spirit,
> that they may be strengthened
> by the gift of your sevenfold grace

The Lex Orandi of the Ordination Rite

for the faithful carrying out
of the work of the ministry.

These are what the Holy Father calls the essential and required words for the valid form of the sacrament. However, it is interesting to note that the rite itself does not indicate them in any special way. The text of the consecratory prayer is approximately fifty lines long, and these half dozen lines simply appear in its course, embedded within the entire Prayer of Ordination. In other words, the sacramental form appears within a longer liturgical prayer that is composed of numerous elements. There is invocation ("*Draw near, we pray, almighty God…*"); praise ("*In your eternal Providence, you make provision for every age…*"); recitation of the *mirabilia Dei* ("*You order all creation.…You grant that the Church, his Body, adorned with manifold heavenly graces…you established three ranks of ministers.…*"); petition ("*We beseech you, Lord: with favor…*"); then the form of the sacrament is spoken, but without pause it is followed by a series of supplications ("*May there abound in them every Gospel virtue.…May your commandments shine forth in their conduct.…May they remain strong and steadfast in Christ.…*"); and finally, there is a trinitarian acclamation of the Lord Jesus who lives and reigns with the Father in the unity of the Holy Spirit, one God.

It seems that the Church has not been content with stating only what is minimally required for validity, but seems to believe that the mystery requires additional expression. One is reminded of what St. Basil said when defending the eucharistic prayer to those who said it could not be found word for word in scripture. Basil replied that some teachings are publicly proclaimed, and others are reserved to members of the household of faith, and among the latter, he names the sign of the cross, praying east, blessing baptismal water, and elements of the eucharistic blessing. He concludes, "As everyone knows, we are not content in the liturgy simply to recite the words recorded by St. Paul or the Gospels, but we add other words both before and after, words of great importance for this mystery."[3] The Church is not content, here, simply to recite the formal words of ordination, but adds other liturgical words and actions and symbols and settings, both before and after the form and matter, which are of great importance for this mystery of the diaconate. We hope now to identify some of these.

The Timing of Ordination

Let us first note when the ordination takes place. We are not only material creatures, we are also temporal ones, and the time assigned for the ordination signifies something. "The Ordination should take place in the presence of as large a gathering of the faithful as possible, on a Sunday or on a feast day, unless pastoral reasons suggest another day" (*Rites of Ordination* 184). This sacrament ordinarily finds its home on the day on which Christians celebrate their resurrection identity. Aidan Kavanagh used to say that Sunday is not a small Easter, but rather that Easter is a big Sunday. What we celebrate once a year in an exceptional manner is a reality normal for us to celebrate every week because it is the constant, eternal source of our temporal life. Robert Taft underscores the significance of Sunday this way:

> To anyone beginning the study of Sunday in early Christian literature, the initial impression is one of confusion: Sunday is the first day, the day of creation, the day of light, the day of the new time. But it is also the last day, the eighth day, the day beyond days, the day of Jubilee, the day of the end-time. It is the day of resurrection, but also the day of the post-resurrection appearances and meals. It is the day of the descent of the Spirit, day of the Ascension, day of the assembly, day of the Eucharist, day of baptism, day of ordinations —until one asks, "Is there *anything* Sunday *doesn't* mean?" The answer, of course, is no. For in the Early Church, Sunday was indeed everything. It was *the* symbolic day, sign of the time of the Church between ascension and parousia, the time in which we are living now. It is the day symbolic of all days, for the purpose of all Christian liturgy is to express in a ritual moment that which should be the basic stance of every moment of our lives.[4]

The rubrics do allow that pastoral reasons can suggest another day, but the symbolism of Sunday identifies the world into which the deacon is stepping. The day of his ordination is the cosmic, eschatological, transfigurative, pneumatic, and ecclesial day, which conditions his entire ministry. And we are expressing, in a ritual moment, something that should become the basic stance of every moment of his life. His entire service of liturgy, Word, and charity should be done in the constant light of this day, with an eschatological note, serving the "Today" that Jesus promised, bringing heaven to earth and earth to heaven. Every Mass celebrates the paschal mystery that calls the Church into being, and it is that mystery the deacon is being ordained to serve.

The Place of Ordination

Where does the ordination take place? "When everything is ready, the procession moves through the Church to the altar in the usual way. Those to be ordained precede the deacon who carries the Book of the Gospels…" (*Rites of Ordination* 193). The train of hierarchical ministers is drawn home to the altar, the *lapis iste*, the stone table of Abel and Jacob and Solomon, which foreshadowed Christ who is the rock of salvation. "When everything is ready," the rubrics note, which presumably means that when a heart has been converted, when a will has acceded, when grace has saturated the ground of one man's life to bring forth shoots of ministry—when all this is ready, and also when the procession is lined up—the altar is approached in the usual way, which is behind the *Book of the Gospels*. The glorious Shekinah of God once led the Israelites by a pillar of fire; the new Israel is led by this Book of Glory. Nearby, the bishop's chair awaits. From this chair he does not act as an individual, but as chief pastor of the diocese. The seat of Moses in the synagogue is now succeeded by the chair of a bishop interpreting and applying the new Law. The one to be ordained wears an alb, a vestment of ministry, reminiscent of the baptismal white garments that clothe each of us in Christ, a foundation garment that can bear the weight of stole and dalmatic.

So we can ask again, Where does the ordination take place? In the bosom of the Church, before the assembly, in the presence of the congregation of the new Israel, at the chair which is occupied by one seated in apostolic succession. The *Catechism of the Catholic Church* describes holy orders as "the sacrament through which the mission entrusted by Christ to his apostles continues to be exercised in the Church until the end of time: thus it is the sacrament of apostolic ministry. It includes three degrees; episcopate, presbyterate, and diaconate" (§ 1536). This is not a personal act by the bishop; it is a sacramental act of apostolic proportion. The bishop will not wield his power arbitrarily or at his own whim, he will do so only because the Church asks him to. To repeat, "Most Reverend Father, holy Mother Church asks you to ordain these men, our brothers, to the responsibility of the diaconate." No ministry is done for its own sake, not even the bishop's ministry of creating new ministers. The Church has seen a need and responded; she has seen a man, and chosen him. Holy Mother Church is a bride who only wishes to please her spouse, and she makes this request to the bishop in obedience to the will of her husband. *Lumen gentium* notes that "for the nurturing and constant growth of the People of God, Christ the Lord instituted in His Church a variety of ministries, which work for the good of the whole body. For those ministers, who are endowed with sacred power, serve their brethren, so that all who are of the People of God, and therefore enjoy a true Christian dignity, working toward a common goal freely and in an orderly way, may arrive at salvation" (LG 18). As a result, and in order to please Jesus, his bride asks the bishop to act.

The Worthiness of the Candidate

That this is the will of God does not mean human beings need not take care; therefore the bishop utilizes all the resources available to him. (Remember that the Church is complex.) He asks the designated priest, "Do you know them to be worthy?" This is not a request for a personal opinion, and the priest does not give one. Instead he testifies, "After inquiry among the Christian people and upon the recommendation of those responsible, I testify that they have been found worthy." The deacon candidates do not come to us as men with no parents, figures of unknown lineage. We may therefore inquire among the people of God about them. Their faith was formed by the body of which they are members. The Apostle Paul says that all the individual members of the Church are connected. The eye cannot say to the hand, or the foot to the head, "I do not need you" (1 Cor 12:21). Therefore, we may ask the eye what it knows about this deacon's hand that will bring viaticum to the dying; we may ask the ear what it knows about this deacon's tongue that will proclaim the Gospel. Further, ask those with even more direct and intimate knowledge of the candidate as a result of having participated in his training. According to the norms that restored the permanent diaconate, candidates should be "received in a special institute where they will be put to the test and will be educated to live a truly evangelical life and prepared to fulfill usefully their own specific functions."[5] Regardless of the fact that it is God's call, God's decision, God's grace at work, we fragile human beings are nonetheless required to put the candidates to the test. These educational institutes are channels through which the Holy Spirit works, and we need not think the activity of the Spirit is better assured when he overflows these channels in an exceptional way.

The Homily

A sample homily is now provided in the rite, one that is intended for two audiences. The bishop "addresses the people and the elect on the office of deacon." Nothing he says should contain any surprises at this point, either to the candidates who have been trained for this, or to the people who hear a rundown of the deacon's ministry. If either is surprised, no one should have let things advance this far. The episcopal preacher is simply summing up the three general areas of ministry to which the candidate is being advanced: Word, altar, and charity. These three are perichoretically related, three atoms united in a single molecular ministry. Sensitive to the fact that the deacon may be married or unmarried, three sets of words are provided, depending on whether married, unmarried, or both married and unmarried elect are to be ordained at this liturgy. The liturgy is adaptable to particular cases.

The Promise from the Elect

A promise from the elect is now requested: "Dear sons, before you enter the Order of the Diaconate, you must declare before the people your intention to undertake this office." This request is made for the same reason that we ask other promises to be made publicly, whether a wedding or the swearing-in of a civil servant. If someone is going to do this ministry, the bishop should know about it, God should know about it, the people should know about it, and the minister himself should be deliberate about it—that's why he makes a declaration of his intention aloud and before the people. He is bringing his decision and his choice into alignment. We sometimes make choices before decisions. Sometimes it is because the urgency of a situation forces a choice out of us before we have had time for full reflection; sometimes it is because of an interior negligence on our part. We choose before we have fully decided; we decide but never get around to choosing. But it should be an objective in life to have choice and decision arrive at the finish tape together, and one purpose of the time given over to diaconal formation is to permit their alignment. We ask the candidates to come to this interior decision, and we ask them to make their choice publicly when they have done so.

The deacon's choice will affect both the present and the future. Consequently, six questions are asked of the candidate: the first about the present moment; the remaining five about future commitments. "Do you resolve to be consecrated for the Church's ministry by the laying on of my hands and the gift of the Holy Spirit?" He must be willing and able. Whether he is *able* to be ordained must already have been answered by canon law, and whether he is *able* to do the ministry expected of him must already have been answered in dialogue with his formators, but at this moment, the bishop is asking if he is *willing* to be consecrated. In astounding respect for our liberty, God asks our permission to grace us. Mary is the model. In a moment, the bishop will call down the Holy Spirit upon this man. Therefore his own *fiat* is requested. If he is so willing, then there are five questions about what he resolves to do: discharge the office with humble charity; hold fast to the mystery of faith with a clear conscience; embrace the celibate state if unmarried; deepen the spirit of prayer; and conform his way of life to the example of Christ—service, belief, prayer, and conversion of life. Be it resolved that he will commit to this, for they are the underpinnings of his ministry.

The deacon will become the hands of the bishop, so it is appropriate that he goes now to place his joined hands between those of the bishop. It is a gesture of respect and obedience, which he now also pledges verbally. There are two reminders that the diaconate is an official ministry of the Church, that is, that it is an office. First, the candidate not only makes this promise of obedience to this particular Ordinary, he also makes it to those who come after. "Do you promise respect and obedience to me *and my successors?*" (*Rites of Ordination* 201). Second, even if the ordaining bishop is not the Ordinary of the candidate, he can nevertheless receive this candidate's promise on behalf of his proper Ordinary. This is a personal pledge, but it is not a pledge to a particular person. Many charisms rise and fall on the breath of the Holy Spirit, but this is not one of those. This has permanence. This is an ecclesiastical office into which the Holy Spirit breathes its support. The Code of Canon Law defines an office as "any function constituted in a stable manner by divine or ecclesiastical ordinance to be exercised for spiritual purpose" (CIC 145). To be an office, a function must be recognized as important for the spiritual life of the Church. The importance of diaconal ministry has been felt since the Book of Acts, and the Latin Church has recently recognized it again with such force as to make some deacons permanent. In any of the three degrees of Orders, the nature of the Church is being sacramentalized, and in the diaconate Order, the Church's heartbeat of *diaconia* (service) is given a face.

The Invitation

We earlier noted the complexity of the Church because it has both visible and invisible dimensions. To confirm the former, "the clergy and other faithful are to be invited to their Ordination so that as many as possible may take part in the celebration" (*Rites of Ordination* 179); to confirm the latter, the litany of supplication is now sung (no. 203). Everyone who has ever lived in the Church is invited to attend; we shall have the dead at our ordinations. What is the assembly's response to the arrival of these holy ones? They add their voice: "Have mercy, pray for us, deliver us, hear our prayer." What are the candidates doing all this time? They have fallen on their faces: "The elect prostrate themselves and the Litany is sung" (no. 203). They lower their countenance to the ground, as Abraham did in Genesis 17, as Moses did in Numbers 16, as Joshua did in chapter 5, as the man with leprosy did in Luke 5, and as Jesus himself did in Gethsemane. Some responses can only be expressed with the body and not by words; some truths must be grasped with the body, and not with the ear. The candidates here do more than they could say. Possible descriptions might include "adoration, supplication, submission, confession of unworthiness, confession of God's glory, begging for mercy, *latreia*." Faith has stretched itself forward; hope has been grounded; ecstatic love has knocked the man off his feet. Earlier rubrics allowed the assembly to have a complete view of the rites, but this is a private moment. The candidate confronts the glory of God that Moses confronted on Mount Sinai, and lacking a veil like Moses had, he hides his face otherwise. While the candidate is in this position, the bishop's words are also humble, praying God to hear the prayers being made and to give help to his own episcopal action: "Graciously accompany with your help what we undertake by virtue of our office. Sanctify by your blessing these men we present, for in our judgment we believe them worthy to exercise sacred ministries" (*Rites of Ordination* 204). He has done all he can; he must now rely upon God's mercy.

The Matter of the Sacrament

The elect rise and go to the bishop who stands at his chair wearing his miter. The matter of the sacrament is applied, reminding us that sacramental matter does not only mean material things like water, bread, and oil. An inward grace is connected to an outward sign in a sacrament, and the outward sign of a sacrament is composed of two essential parts, namely, thing and Word. And the thing is either a physical substance, or an action perceptible to the senses. The matter of the sacrament of ordination is the laying on of hands. Such an action in the Bible is one of blessing, consecration, transmission, commissioning, strengthening. In full view of the assembly, the bishop lays his hands upon the head of each candidate, without saying anything. The prayer of ordination will follow in just a moment, but first silence—simply action.

Form now determines the application of matter as noted by Pius XII, who concludes that the words spoken as the form of the sacrament "unequivocally signify the sacramental effects—namely, the power of orders and the grace of the Holy Spirit—and are accepted and used as such by the Church."[6] The effects of this sacramental outburst by God deserve consideration. The effect of this sacrament is a power and a grace. The scholastic theologians defined power as "an ability to act." We have already seen that the prayer in which the matter and form are found contains numerous parts: invocation, praise, *mirabilia dei*, petition, supplication, and doxology. As a whole, the prayer connects the present activity of God to his past activity in the salvation history of his people Israel. God remains unchanged but makes all things new, and makes provision for every age. He does so by apportioning every order and assigning every office. God once chose the sons of Levi to minister in the tabernacle; now God establishes three ranks of ministers. God adorns the Church, his Body, with manifold heavenly graces so that she will grow and spread forth to build up a new temple. To serve that Church, Christ's apostles appointed seven men of good repute to assist them in the daily ministry. The ministry of serving at table was entrusted to these seven by the apostles' prayer and laying on of hands; in the same way, the bishop will now dedicate these servants of God to the office of deacon so they may minister at God's holy altar.

The Epiclesis

Thus we arrive at the form which is called "essential and required for validity." It is an epiclesis, which by definition is both human petition and divine consent. In any epiclesis, we beg the Lord God to send the Holy Spirit so that certain graces may be ours. An epiclesis makes something holy by contact with God. The *Catechism* says confidently that the Father always hears the prayer of his Son's Church, and that in a sacramental epiclesis, the Church "expresses her faith in the power of the Spirit. As fire transforms into itself everything it touches, so the Holy Spirit transforms into the divine life whatever is subjected to his power" (CCC 1127). Things that are touched by this fire become oriented toward particular sacramental effects. So it is in the epicleses of baptism, confirmation, and Eucharist: the Spirit comes upon the water so those buried in it can rise to newness of life; he comes upon the confirmand to give freedom from sin, and himself as helper and guide; he comes upon the bread and wine to make them the body and blood of Christ, and those who eat it into one body and one spirit. So it also is in the epiclesis of ordination. Why does this fire touch the deacon? It is not merely a matter of commissioning him with functional tasks. If that was all it is then the bishop could handle it alone. Rather, the deacon is being given a supernatural character, and for that we need the Holy Spirit's action. This is not about *doing*, rather about *becoming*. The deacon will live this tension between doing and being, it is true, and he must never forget that his servant activity comes from having been modeled after Christ the Servant. He has been made a symbol, model, icon of Christ. When people see the future ministry of the deacon, they should be able to see through it to wonder at the source of that ministry. Then beauty will attract, and the deacon will become an evangelical man for being pneumatically imprinted with the image of Christ. He becomes charismatic.

The prayer identifies the gifts we ask the Holy Spirit to bestow. Give him strength to carry out the work of the ministry. Without being strengthened by sevenfold heavenly graces, his ministry would be nothing beyond what natural man can do; without being inflated by the divine breath, the ministry would be flaccid; without an epiclesis that brings power from heaven, he would be a social organizer but not a divine minister. We pray the Spirit to give him every gospel virtue in abundance: "unfeigned love, concern for the sick and poor, unassuming authority, the purity of innocence, and the observance of spiritual discipline." The diaconate is a vocation, and in kingdom vocations, the deacon must himself become what he is serving. The love and compassion and purity that come from Christ must make the deacon loving and compassionate and pure as they flow through him. The pipe should be changed by the liquid it conveys; the deacons are changed by the grace of Christ that flows through them. The result will be that deacons will "shine forth in their conduct, so that by the example of their way of life they may inspire the imitation of your holy people." The bestowed diaconal character will be manifested through action, but it will be manifested through action so that it can be imitable.

The Holy Spirit will be putting speech in his mouth for his ministry of word, animating his hands for his ministry of charity, and taking residence in his heart for his ministry of the altar. Only thus will the deacon become a spiritual man, a man of the Spirit, the same Spirit who works always with the Son, and so the prayer concludes that he will in this life imitate the Son, who came to serve, and not to be served.

The Signs of Ordination

The deacon receives two signs of the ordination that has occurred. First is the outward vesture of stole and dalmatic, during which may be sung Psalm 84: "How lovely is your dwelling place, O LORD of hosts..../ My home is by your altars..../ Blessed are those who dwell in your house!" (vv. 1–5). He has come home. His future ministry must derive its strength from contact with the Lord's altar, the throne of God. The deacon will conduct much of his ministry beyond the walls of the Church, that is true, but he will never lose contact with the thread that connects him to the courts of the Lord. He receives a second sign of his ordination, the *Book of the Gospels* "whose herald you have become." This book will rest in physical contact with the altar during the liturgy, but it is also meant to be a traveling book. The Jewish Torah to this day is kept in a traveling cover, ready for pilgrimage at a moment's notice. This Gospel will be brought to many surprised people by a deacon. He will herald the gospel in places that the bishop and presbyter do not reach. In handing over the Gospel book, the bishop gives a riddle worthy of a fairytale: "Believe what you read, teach what you believe, and practice what you teach." The mind fingers the knot to see how these are tied together, and in so doing discovers again the threefold ministry of the deacon: believe what you read and proclaim in the *liturgy*, teach in your ministry of *Word* what you have come to believe, and practice in *charity* what you teach. It is not enough to do it without becoming it. He is not merely a reader, he must believe; he is not merely a teacher, he must become the gospel in the core of his being.

Transition to the Mass

The rite ends with a fraternal kiss between bishop and new deacon, and transitions to the Order of Mass. But this Mass will open up to accommodate new ministers within it: the new deacons bring the offerings and assist the bishop at the altar, and the eucharistic prayers take notice of their new presence. The first Eucharistic Prayer states,

> Therefore, Lord, we pray:
> graciously accept this oblation of our service,
> that of your whole family,
> which we make to you
> also for your servants
> whom you have been pleased to raise to the Order
>   of the Diaconate.

The second, third, and fourth Eucharistic Prayers mention them explicitly during the prayer for clergy:

> Remember, Lord, your Church,
> spread throughout the world,
> and bring her to the fullness of charity,
> together with N. our Pope
> and N. our Bishop.
> Be mindful also of these your servants,
> whom you have willed to provide today as ministers
>   for the Church,

and all the clergy.
Remember also our brothers and sisters…

Acknowledging that the deacons were formed in faith by families of faith, their parents and relatives may receive communion under both kinds, and the deacons themselves assist the bishop in giving communion to the faithful. At the concluding rite, a tripartite blessing is given, reminding the newly ordained deacons that they have been called to service (so we ask God to give him zeal for all, especially the afflicted and poor), entrusting them with preaching the gospel (so we ask God to help him be a sincere and fervent witness in our lives according to God's Word), and appointing them as stewards of God's mysteries (so we ask God to make him an imitator of Jesus and a minister of unity and peace).

CONCLUSION

Based on our examination of this ordination rite, the sacramental character and ministry of the deacon is fourfold.

The deacon is a complex man. It is Christ's Church that the deacon will serve, and it is a complex Church. He must be called by holy Mother Church, who is the one who asks the bishop to ordain these men. She does so in submission to her spouse. There is no trace of entrepreneurship here. This is not a ministry that he creates for himself, for giving oneself a vocation (call) would be an odd sort of ventriloquism. The deacon does not choose between serving the hierarchical, visible, earthly society and the spiritual, invisible, heavenly enriched mystical body. He must serve them both. He is a man of the Church, and so serves one complex reality coalesced from a divine and human element, which means we will find him in the mystical and the mundane, as at home in the spiritual as he is in the street.

The deacon is a man of mystery. This is not a phrase for the beginning of a detective novel. Rather, it is the phrase Ignatius used: the deacons are ministers of the mysteries of Jesus Christ. Jesus is the mystery of God made known in the flesh, and the deacon resolves to further conform his way of life to the example of Christ, to hold fast to the mystery of faith with a clear conscience, to deepen his life of prayer, all so he can discharge his office in humble charity. He is a minister filled with the mystery he serves, and the mystery of Jesus is hypostatic and paschal.

The deacon is a spiritual man. The matter of this sacrament is epicletic, which means he becomes a man of the Spirit. Being a spiritual man does not mean an ethereal, ghostly man; it means being a man filled with the third person of the Trinity. To be spiritual means to belong to the Holy Spirit, which he now does. What was the work of the Spirit in the mystery of the incarnation? By the power of the third person of the Trinity, the second person of the Trinity became incarnate of the Virgin Mary. What is the work of the Spirit in the mystery of the diaconate? The same effect: to bring the Word of God into the world. The Holy Spirit descended like a dove upon Jesus at his baptism to begin his public ministry, and so he has done for the deacon, sacramentally, in order to go with him into his public ministry.

The deacon is a bilocating man. The tradition has understood the architecture of the Church to be tripartite: sanctuary, nave, and narthex. The sanctuary represents heaven, the nave represents the ark of the Church, and the narthex represents the world. The narthex is the threshold between sacred and profane, meeting in the nave like a freshwater river mingles with the saltwater sea. From the throne of Christ comes the river of liturgy, we are told in the Book of Revelation, and this river flows outward into the great ocean of life. The deacon's special arena of ministry is the narthex, which is the membrane between Church and world. He stands with one foot in the sacred and one foot in the profane, bilocated, ushering Christians into the sacred and accompanying Christians in the profane. He is a mediator, which means an ordained minister of the Church. He unites the ministries of altar, word, and charity. He rides that river of liturgy from the altar to the street outside, which he serves by rubbing shoulders with the people of God in their secular life. He climbs the mount of Zion while drawing people from the streets and byways of the world to the source of eternal life, which he serves at the altar.

NOTES

1. Apostolic Constitution Laying Down Certain Norms regarding the Holy Order of Deacons, quoting Ignatius, *Ad Magnesios* 4.

2. (*Emitte in eos Domine, quaesumus, Spiriturn Sanctum, quo in opus ministerii fideliter exsequendi munere septiformis tuae gratiae roborentur*). See: http://www.ewtn.com/library/PAPALDOC/P6ORDIN.HTM.

3. Cf. Basil on the Holy Spirit.

4. Robert Taft, "Sunday in the Byzantine Tradition," in *Beyond East and West: Problems in Liturgical Understanding*, 2nd ed. (Rome: Pontifical Oriental Institute, 1997), 52.

5. *Sacrum diaconatus ordinem* 6.

6. Pius XII, *Sacramentum ordinis*, quoted by Paul VI in *Apostolic Constitutions*.

7.

Identity and Holiness

JAMES KEATING

Although some functions of a deacon, especially in missionary countries, are entrusted to laymen, it is nevertheless "beneficial that those who perform a truly diaconal ministry be *strengthened by the imposition of hands*, a tradition going back to the apostles, and be *more closely joined to the altar* so that they may more effectively carry out their ministry *through the sacramental grace of the diaconate*." The diaconate is adorned with its own indelible character and its own special grace so that those who are called to it "can permanently serve the mysteries of Christ and the Church."[1]

The deacon is a man who is rendered permanently available to the servant mysteries of Christ through ordination; he is one *opened* to Christ by the "wound" of this sacramental character.[2] These servant mysteries inhere within the larger paschal mystery of Christ's own bodily self-donation for the salvation of the world unto death and resurrection. Jesus' life is a mission in obedience to the Father's desire that "none be lost" (John 6:39) and that his "home may be filled" (Luke 14:23). This mission is a self-emptying (*kenosis*) that is ordered toward reconciliation, healing, and service to those who are in need. For deacons who welcome grace, this self-emptying is not attained by the presence of any natural empathy in their hearts. Rather, it is accomplished by a grace-filled surrender of the whole body in communion with Christ's own self-gift. For the deacon who moves within this grace, his ego is decentered rendering him available to give. Grace enables the body, in real and complete actions of freedom, to host Christ's own mission. This is true because the way of the diaconate in each new epoch is one of incarnating the eager availability of Christ to serve the deepest human needs. The deacon's mission is to keep "the circle of charity turning,"[3] both sacramentally and through his ministerial mission. In this, the deacon sacramentalizes the mission of Christ the servant and his Church. The deacon's identity becomes a mission.

> St. Stephen is a model for all those who want to serve the new evangelization. He shows that the novelty of proclamation does not primarily consist in the use of original methods or techniques, which certainly have their uses, but in being filled with the Holy Spirit and allowing ourselves to be guided by him. The novelty of proclamation lies in immersing ourselves deeply in the mystery of Christ, the assimilation of his Word and of his presence in the Eucharist, *so that he himself, the living Jesus, can act and speak through his envoy.*[4]

To be a deacon is to be one who comes from and exists in communion with the servant mysteries of Christ. The deacon lives in the reality of being obedient to the sending agent, Christ in the person of the bishop. It is adherence to this obedient sending *in Christ* that both defines the deacon and spiritually constitutes him in diaconal dependency: "as I have done for you, you should also do" (John 13:15). Such dependence upon *Christ's own actions operating within him* is the hidden power from which a deacon draws as the bishop sends him into ministry. This dependence upon grace is the treasure of Christ's *own* obedience, now being shared with the deacon through the sacred character of ordination: "a son cannot do anything on his own, but only what he sees his father doing" (John 5:19). Paradoxically, with such dependency upon or through a better union with Christ comes a certain ministerial creativity. Such creativity is as wide and deep as a deacon's obedience to the mission Christ gives him, a mission that seeks to imbue the paschal mystery deeper into culture. For the deacon, his obedience to Christ, dependency upon him, and union with him all yield "newness" (Isa 43:19; Rev 21:5; 2 Cor 5:17) as opposed to ego independence, which only draws from the limits of the self, thus yielding boredom and repetition.[5]

The dependency upon Christ's own obedience that a deacon lives out is in accord with the meaning of the term *deacon* itself. *Diakon-* words are associated with actions that manifest a mission, that is, a deacon is a man who is sent *by another*. The deacon is an *envoy* who speaks not on his own authority but by the authority of the one who sent him.[6] The content of what a deacon does is not defined by his title; in fact, what a deacon does is indeterminate and needs to be discerned while he stands in the presence of God, listening to him and awaiting his mission.[7] What Christ is sharing with the deacon at ordination is *his own obedience* in carrying out his assignment from the Father. This assignment was to reconcile all things to himself through and by the incarnation. Christ is sent by the Father to bind up wounds, preach the truth, and offer himself up in love for the sake of others. It is crucial for the deacon to internalize the truth of his vocation as constituting the continuation of Christ's own obedience, raptly listening to the Father as one who is sent. To this end, Pope Benedict XVI broadens the popular understanding of the deacon from one who directly serves the economically poor to a more expansive role as a sacred messenger:

> In these years *new forms of poverty* have emerged…. Indeed, many people have lost the meaning of life and do not possess a truth upon which to build their existence; a great many young people ask to meet men and women who can listen to and advise them in life's difficulties. Besides material poverty, we also find spiritual and cultural poverty….Be *servants of the Truth* in order to be *messengers of the joy* that God desires to give to every human being.[8]

Here, Pope Benedict XVI does not limit the deacon's ministry to the materially poor, but creatively places it within a broader field of mission. The deacon is to cultivate an imagination that takes him to the heart of human need, not simply to the nearest charity that attends to material deprivation. This same pope also invites us to consider a more innovative and accurate image of the deacon—that of envoy. This identity is noted within his meditation upon the life of deacon St. Stephen: "The novelty of proclamation [of the new evangelization by deacons] lies in immersing ourselves deeply in the mystery of Christ, the assimilation of His Word and of His presence in the Eucharist, so that He Himself, the living Jesus, can act and speak *through His envoy*."[9]

The living Jesus acts through his deacons; their words are one. Analogically, through obedience to the bishop, the deacon as his envoy becomes effective in ministry only when the bishop's word and the acts of the deacon are *one*: "I only do what I see the Father doing" (see John 5:19); "I and the Father are one" (John 10:30).[10] Deacons participate in the servant mysteries of Christ; therefore, their being is empowered by the grace of ordination *to become responsive* to Christ's Word as carried in the office of the bishop. Deeper still, diaconal obedience develops in the course of a man's own spiritual maturation, which blossoms into a true liberation. The deacon *wants* the servant mysteries of Christ to *possess* him, *define* him, and in the end, *purify* him. Having such an interior life attracts the deacon to Christ even more; Christ will be his only desire. Diaconal obedience, therefore, "becomes the external expression of one's deepest desire…the will of the other [God-bishop] remains distinct from one's own and yet becomes the very heart of one's own willing."[11]

The deacon's cry, then, is "Here I am…send me!" (Isa 6:8). The only way a deacon can have an "identity" crisis is if he forgets who chose him and who sent him: Christ through the bishop. For the deacon, his way of obedience *is* a way of communion, a way of secured unity with Christ that yields readied self-giving. The diaconal identity is therefore a mission flowing from a relationship of trust in the authority of truth, trust that the bishop listens to the love-imbued truth of God's own Son. As Hans Urs von Balthasar noted, our understanding of being sent is intrinsic to the very concept of who a person is: "We are to assimilate our own 'I' more and more completely to our God-given mission and to discover in this mission our own identity, which is both personal and social."[12] The deacon acquires his mission by his relationship to the mission of Christ and his servant mysteries. In order for a deacon to become holy, he must *not* resist the mission that is *becoming his identity* in and through the communion he has with Christ, the bishop, and the Church. The deacon embraces this obedient life because he recognizes that such a "way" of living is "his" way to stay in communion with the Trinity. Therefore, such obedience is a "light burden" (Matt 11:30). Like Christ, in his obedience, the deacon will be *beautiful in his actions*, actions that flow from his ecclesially based communion with God. Such beauty is glimpsed in Luke 14 as the "Lord" sends his "deacon" to the highways in order to "compel" people to come and fill his house (14:23 NRSV). The deacon compels others to the eucharistic banquet, not by threats, force, or external compulsion of any kind, but by the radiance of the truth manifested in his persuasive acts of service,[13] for beauty not only attracts, it informs. One is attracted to beauty because it carries both the promise of affective fulfillment and the content of truth.[14] By way of these acts, the deacon reveals the source of his own authority and within such acts of charity, instruction, or counsel, it becomes evident to those outside such communion that the deacon is to be reckoned with: "Let's listen to this man *as he is sent*." This identity compels because there is congruency between the deacon's communion with the source and his actions. The deacon reveals a kind of obedience that discloses a love freely given from God and freely received by the deacon.[15] The disclosure of such love by the deacon's *actions* reveals the origin to be his communion with the Trinity. It is this source that flows through him and "waters," refreshes, and attracts the lives of others.[16] However, before he attracts others, he must first position himself in vulnerability to the attractive pull of divine beauty. This "position" is one of hospitality toward the grace that transforms and purifies desire into self-gift.[17] In fact, this is what diaconal formation is about, the purification and reorientation of desire (*eros*) so that one no longer worships the culture of distraction, but is attracted finally to the actions of Christ upon the cross. In such purification, the deacon becomes a man who listens for and to all who carry pain. He can only become "one who listens and is sent" if he continually surrenders himself to God, which does not threaten the self, but enables him to possess the self even more fully in freedom. In this surrender, the deacon experiences his "self" as "his" to give away in the service of the Word.[18] Surrender leads to true self-donation, authentic gift giving.

THE SERVANT MYSTERIES OF CHRIST

For one who listens, the actions of Christ become the only actions worthy of contemplation. Such contemplation becomes intrinsic to the deacon's life so that the actions of Christ fill his imagination and strengthen resistance against temptations to return to a life of cultural distraction. However, such contemplation is not an end in itself for deacons nor for the Church in its *servant core*.[19] In his conscience—his heart[20]—a deacon listens to Christ, beholds Christ's own actions in prayer, and is then sent by his conscience into action. Action originates in the *truths known in the ecclesially formed conscience, which then becomes a source of mission*. Therefore, the center of diaconal conscience formation is not an isolated "I," but *Christ's own actions* as they manifest themselves in the Church's worship and sacraments. Contemplating these actions in the conscience, the heart and seat of decision making, they bind the deacon to the truth, the truth *to be done* with, and only with, Christ. Hence, the deacon has become free by being bound (John 15:5).

All those who long for God are longing for union with him. Desire for such union is the true orientation of the person whose aim is holiness. In the case of the deacon, as with all specified vocations, he does not simply long for God in some generic sense—"this holiness of the Church is unceasingly manifested, and…is expressed in many ways in individuals,"[21]—he longs for God within a specific desire: that Christ again lives in him as the delegation from the Father. The deacon's form of holiness is commensurate with the vocation itself. Therefore, the deacon's desire to define his conscience through the servant mysteries of Christ *is* Christ's own desire for the deacon as well. The one who is sent, Christ, is sharing his own *diakonia* with the deacon in obedience to his mission from the Father. *In Christ*, our obedience extinguishes the distance between us, who tend toward sin, and the holiness that is God.[22]

The servant mysteries of Christ are those actions of Jesus revealed in scripture (for example, Luke 10:29ff.; 14:15-23; 17:7-10; 22:27; John 13:14-15) that embody his own self-donative mission.[23] If authentic, the call to diaconate is Christ choosing a man, his particular body. So, as noted above, Christ desires to live his own servant mysteries over again within the deacon's body. This living over again is not simply the result of being baptized; all are called to holiness by the indwelling of the Holy Spirit. No, this "living over again" configures a man to the interior identity of Christ in the particularity of his own servanthood in such a way that the ministerial acts of a deacon begin from, and remain in union with, these same servant mysteries. Being configured to Christ's own delegated identity is so distinct that it is a new sacrament beyond baptism. Jesus Christ defines himself as "I am among you as the one who serves" (Luke 22:27), and he is still among us in the form of the diaconal charism, which is not reducible to social service, as it contains an allusion to the sacred.[24] The sending of the Son and the Son's obedience to being sent are the most mysterious of realities. In the mission of Christ, in "going out" to the lost, we find the fullest expression of *who* the person of Christ is. A deacon's desire to "go and do likewise" (Luke 10:37) has its origin in Christ's own erotic nature as he is urged on to do the will of the Father. He shares this urgent longing to obey with men in holy orders. The two sayings of Christ: "Go and do likewise" and "I have given you a model to follow, so that *as I have done for you, you should also do*. Amen, amen, I say to you, no slave is greater than his master *nor any messenger greater than the one who sent him*" (John 13:15-16; author's emphasis), both encapsulate the diaconal mission and become touchstones for diaconal identity. Each man must remain in prayer to ascertain if he, in fact, is being sent or if he has usurped his place as *messenger* and become the *agent* who sends. Christ's longing to see that his Father's house is full (Luke 14:23) is instantiated in his "going out" and searching for the lost (Matt 15:24; Luke 15:1-32), but his going and searching is always the result of being sent. The diaconate is this dominical mission sacramentalized. Deacons desire to be affected by Christ's obedience and his longing by the Lord. In fact, they should ask him to receive a portion of such longing. In this way, the deacon is called to enter the prayer of Christ so that the Lord's desires become his own. "The person who has beheld Jesus' intimacy with his Father and has come to understand him *from within* is called to be a 'rock' of the Church. *The Church arises out of participation in the prayer of Jesus* (cf. Luke 9:18-20; Matt 16:13-20)."[25] If the Church arises from such participation, then certainly the "sacramentalized" service embodied in the deacon does as well. Those in holy orders enflesh the Lord's evangelical longings and extend this mission to where it has yet to reach.

THE DEACON, PRAYER, AND HOLINESS

The deacon, who enfleshes these longings, catches the fire of holiness as secured through the Holy Spirit, for it is the Spirit of Christ who gifts the deacon with involvement in the eternal relation that is God.[26] In extending these relations to the deacon, God's desire is "fulfilled" and the deacon's desires now rest in his new identity as defined at the Second Vatican Council:

> Ministers of lesser rank are also sharers in the mission and grace of the Supreme Priest. In the first place among these ministers are deacons, who, in as much as they are dispensers of Christ's mysteries and servants of the Church, should keep themselves free from every vice and stand before men as personifications

of goodness and friends of God. Clerics, who are called by the Lord and are set aside as His portion in order to prepare themselves for the various ministerial offices under the watchful eye of spiritual shepherds, are bound to bring their hearts and minds into accord with this special election (which is theirs). They will accomplish this by their constancy in prayer, by their burning love, and by their unremitting recollection of whatever is true, just and of good repute. They will accomplish all this for the glory and honor of God.[27]

According to the Church, a deacon will bring his vocation to fulfillment by way of constant prayer, burning love, and ceaseless recollection. All of these characteristics pertain to his inner life. The interior life secures the life of self-donation and helps a man hold fast to the mission of being one *who is sent*. This vocation, then, demands an *eager availability to the call of God* as reflected in the words used by the Second Vatican Council—"*constancy* in prayer," "*burning love*," and "*unremitting recollection*"! In each of these dispositions, a man is entering the mystery of "liturgical asceticism," the life of Christ lived in us.[28] The deacon wants Christ's life to ignite his desire to be with God in a constant, burning, and recollected way. This description does not reveal a vocation that is "hobby" like, but one that is all-consuming, one that defines. Such a vocation requires the deacon's daily consent to *be taken* on behalf of others' needs.[29] An ascetical feature is therefore necessary in diaconal formation and life. This feature would facilitate a man's losing interest in the culture of distraction—that is, the Western popular culture—while simultaneously deepening his hospitality toward Christ as his deepest attraction and commitment.[30] It is not "natural" to find Christ attractive because men have become "full" of the satisfactions and meanings endemic to popular, political, and economic culture. These interests weigh so heavily upon the contemporary man's commitments that Christ first appears as a threat and not a promise. Even for those who are attracted to holy orders, the anticipation of being weaned from the superficial consolations of Western culture can, at first, be negatively received. Formation in holy orders as a formation in asceticism frees a man to participate in the paschal mystery and is essential in ordering a man toward the holy.

Foundationally then, the *holy* is God's own nature and life—the holy is love itself. We say the word *love* with such familiarity, but in fact divine love is mostly mystery, mostly that which we can experience through faith in Christ, but never exhaust as "known," as knowledge "mastered." "Holiness" *from a human perspective* is always experienced as *more to receive*, more to engage as the holy arrests the human person and beguiles him, moving the mind and heart beyond the one he now possesses. Holiness is a disposition of the heart that moves a person to profound trust in *God's goodness*, not *one's own*.[31] The *fruit* of such trust is a life of charity, and yet we must still recognize our natural tendency to put a claim on God by accumulating a life of ethical "successes."[32] God dismisses this as a distortion of holiness by the very truth of his divine nature. Holiness is *given*, shared, but not earned.

Through faith, hope, and love, the Christian is moved toward God by God in order to participate in this eternal love in and through the power of Christ. Once one believes in the mystery of the Blessed Trinity as revealed by Christ, one can then discern all things within a new imagination. This imagination is sacred, born of faith, born of surrender to Christ. Each vocation specifies and particularizes this imagination and, through it, this new way of being grasped by reality, that Christ reaches the mind of the deacon. Specifically, Christ produces and reaches the diaconal mind by affecting him with his own servant mysteries.[33] The *experience of being moved by these mysteries* opens up the possibility of a diaconal imagination. Only when one has experienced these mysteries as *real*, does the mind conspire with the affect for new imagery.[34] Without the experience of being taken up into these mysteries, there can be no real entry into a new culture, noted for its diminishing interest in the distractions of this passing age (Rom 12:1-2).

Those who are permeable to the paschal mystery receive their vocation as an invitation and not simply as a moral example. Living within the mystery is the very condition that makes it possible to become "one who is sent." As this mystery is heard and received, a man partakes in the universal call to holiness but without the specificity of imparting a personal diaconal imagination. Recognizing a specific call from Christ, a man is then ushered into a particular reality. From this he is formed in, and comes to possess and cultivate, a new imagination—one that is diaconal in identity and behavior. In the diaconal way of holiness, not only is a man's love of his vocation deepened, but his loving fidelity to *this particular call* to holiness opens up the entire meaning of his life (inclusive of marriage, labor, friendships, moral development, and so forth). The universal, the full meaning of his life, is attained through the particular doorway of holy orders. "All the faithful, whatever their condition or state, are called by the Lord, *each in his own way*, to that perfect holiness whereby the Father Himself is perfect."[35]

God stoops down to *call us particularly* so that our *entire being* can be raised up to participate in his own mysterious, consoling love. Because it arises from a deacon's own communion with the servant mysteries of Christ, inhering as they do in this definitive statement: "I came down from heaven *not to do my own will but the will of the one who sent me*" (John 6:38; 4:34; author's emphasis), the diaconal imagination should be aflame with bold, prophetic action for each age. To be one who is sent is the diaconal identity of Christ; he wills to share it with the men he calls to holy orders. It is *this identity* that gracefully informs a deacon's imagination and facilitates his taking on the mind of Christ (1 Cor 2:16). Such a *metanoia*, however, is not simply due to one's personal devotion to Christ the servant; it is also secured because the diaconate is an *ecclesial vocation*, and as such, it *paradoxically* establishes the *personal holiness* of the deacon. The ecclesial and objective nature of Christ's call is expressed when the bishop elects a man, and hence personal holiness progresses only within the ecclesial structure that assists a man not to do his *own* will.

> Ordination consequently not only means a mission and authority received from Christ to act in his place: it also means authority and power to act *in persona ecclesiae* as a permanent servant of the Church. This

power is also sacramental and symbolic. That is: acting not in place of the Church as if he were someone delegated by it—we are not in the juridical sphere!—but as that *organ* through which and in which the Church is present and acting.[36]

Therefore, in order for a deacon to do the will of the "one who sent me," he has to stay deeply rooted in relationships that carry the truth of who God is and what his Church is accomplishing in grace. These relationships include a man's own prayer life, the bishop and his agents, and various members of the Church who form a diaconal candidate, especially a spiritual director.[37] Of course, all these relationships continue after ordination as well. Diaconal holiness, then, is received within the depths of contemplative prayer regarding the servant mysteries of Christ, in the Church's ministry of the deacon in Sacrament and Word, in his own commitment to spiritual direction, in the grace of marriage (if it applies), and in the grace of that circulation of love that is his ministry and manifested desire.

CONCLUSION

The classes and duties of life are many, but holiness is one—that sanctity which is cultivated by all who are moved by the Spirit of God, and who obey the voice of the Father and worship God the Father in spirit and in truth.

Ministers of lesser rank are also sharers in the mission and grace of the Supreme Priest. In the first place among these ministers are deacons, who, in as much as they are dispensers of Christ's mysteries and servants of the Church, should keep themselves free from every vice and stand before men as personifications of goodness and friends of God....They will accomplish this by their constancy in prayer, by their burning love, and by their unremitting recollection of whatever is true, just and of good repute. They will accomplish all this for the glory and honor of God.[38]

Holiness is one, but it is expressed in *incarnational ways* according to the mission given to each person by God. The deacon is a man who regards the development of interiority as primary, yet embraces an inexorably paradoxical truth: *interior development leaves him no choice but to freely engage the culture by continuing the mission of Christ*. Diaconal holiness is not reflected in a rush of ministerial "workaholism," an anthem of unreflective service to the economically poor. The deacon's holiness is intrinsically linked to his spiritual and moral leadership—leadership recognized by the bishop and respected by the persons so served. The deacon, first and foremost, is sent because he has encountered the love of the Trinity and is sustained by it. This encounter, which carries a mission, is ratified by the bishop's consecration, is deepened by the deacon's immersion in the Word of God; is suffered by his receiving the truth about his moral and spiritual maturation, and is made fruitful by his service to others as he has been served by Christ's own mission.

Diaconal holiness is received as a gift from the Trinity so that the love of many will *not* grow cold (Matt 24:12). "All that is necessary is that love which is the substance of the Church, the sacraments, and all of God's words and laws, should be continually flowing from his prayer straight into action."[39] The deacon, an envoy of Christ, is sent from the heart of the Church (the altar) to deeply embed himself within the secular world with the life-giving message of salvation. As each deacon labors to announce the good news, he does so with the assurance that a charism is given to him. This charism is primarily one of a cleric living a lay life. It is a charism that enables him to be "consecrated," set aside, but only so that he might become more deeply involved in the character of the ordinary.

He serves primarily by being vulnerable to receiving grace himself, by being open to receiving divine intimacy in his heart, so that such intimacy may define his presence. The deacon becomes eager to say, "I have to give myself in Christ's own self-gift. The power is Christ's; the cooperation with such power is my gift to him." In the deacon, the Lord desires to be with his people in their need, and the deacon cooperates with this dominical desire by facilitating the circulation of charity in the midst of work, health care, law, education, labor, and more.

As Christ descends upon the deacon at ordination, he is also descending upon the culture through the diaconal ministry. The paradoxical tension of a cleric living a lay life is a purposeful charism, and the deacon ought never to attempt to relax its inherent tension by either downplaying his role at the altar or ignoring his spiritual leadership role within the larger community. His holiness depends upon a faithful execution of service by one who is "joined to the altar" and an "envoy to the culture" from Christ.

NOTES

1. Paul VI, *Motu Propio* on the General Norms for Restoring the Permanent Diaconate in the Latin Church *Sacrum Diaconatus Ordinem* (June 18, 1967), no. 5. (Author's emphasis.)

2. "In the 14th century, in the book *The Life in Christ* by the Byzantine theologian, Nicholas Cabasilas, we rediscover Plato's experience in which the ultimate object of nostalgia, transformed by the new Christian experience, continues to be nameless. Cabasilas says: 'When men have a longing so great that it surpasses human nature and eagerly desire and are able to accomplish things beyond human thought, it is the Bridegroom who has smitten them with this longing. It is he who has sent a ray of his beauty into their eyes. The greatness of the wound already shows the arrow which has struck home, the longing indicates who has inflicted the wound' (cf. *The Life in Christ*, the Second Book, 15)." Ratzinger quotes this comment within his meditation on what effects beauty has upon a man. Because Christ is beauty (the radiation of truth) itself, this quotation perfectly reflects what happens to a man in receiving the sacramental character. Christ "wounds" the candidate with the beauty of his being and mission, summoning the deacon to receive his identity and mission from within the beauty of the servant mysteries of Christ. See http://www.vatican.va/roman_curia/congregations/cfaith/documents/rc_con_cfaith_doc_20020824_ratzinger-cl-rimini_en.html. It is also helpful to look at the sacramental character from the point of view of *receptivity*. At ordination, one does not simply receive an abstract commission

to "serve," but one suffers the activity of something good. This good reality, a life of participating in the servant mysteries of Christ through grace, changes the one who "suffers" this goodness. He welcomes such an affect and surrenders to its beauty and truth, welcoming his new defining constitution. The man *becomes* a deacon. He becomes one who bears the mystery of Christ's own mission within his flesh. One can see the power of ordination by analogously reflecting upon it in light of God's giving of himself in creation: "Without in any way diminishing his own being the divine lover leaves himself, passing into the object of his love in such a way that his goodness leaves an *imprint* concretely in history, arousing *a real change* and a sense of affinity *on the part of those who encounter and suffer its beauty*" (Adam G. Cooper, *Holy Eros: A Liturgical Theology of the Body* (Kettering, OH: Angelico Press, 2014), 18–23. (Author's emphasis.) This is what happens at ordination as well.

3. Guy Mansini expresses the deacon's role this way in several unpublished correspondences with this author.

4. Benedict XVI, *Angelus* (December 26, 2012). (Author's emphasis.)

5. "As God is unconditionally the master of our thinking as of our acting, rationality and obedience cannot be opposed, being one in their root" (Louis Bouyer, "The Permanent Relevance of John Henry Newman," in *The Proceedings of the Wethersfield Institute* (San Francisco: Ignatius, 1988).

6. See Karl Paul Donfried, "Ministry: Rethinking the Term *Diakonia*," *Concordia Theological Quarterly* 56, no. 1 (January): 1–15; and John N. Collins, *Diakonia Studies* (Oxford: Oxford University Press, 2014).

7. Collins, *Diakonia Studies*, 82–83.

8. Benedict XVI, Address to the Permanent Deacons of Rome (February 18, 2006). (Author's emphasis.)

9. Benedict XVI, "Weekly Angelus" (December 26, 2012).

10. "Let everyone revere the deacons as Jesus Christ, the bishop *as the image of the Father*, and the presbyters as the senate of God and the assembly of the apostles. For without them one cannot speak of the Church." See *Catechism of the Catholic Church*, 2nd ed. (Washington, DC: United States Catholic Conference, 2000), no. 1554, quoting Saint Ignatius of Antioch. (Author's emphasis.)

11. Mark McIntosh, *Mystical Theology* (Oxford: Blackwell, 1998), 110.

12. Hans Urs von Balthasar, *Theo-Drama: Theological Dramatic Theory III* (San Francisco: Ignatius Press, 1992), 270ff.

13. Hans Urs von Balthasar, *The Glory of the Lord: A Theological*

Aesthetics, vol. 1, *Seeing the Form* (San Francisco: Ignatius Press, 1982), 118.

14. Romanus Cessario, *Theology and Sanctity* (Ave Maria, FL: Sapientia Press, 2014), 30.

15. Hans Urs von Balthasar, *Engagement with God* (San Francisco: Ignatius Press, 2008), 78.

16. John Crosby, *The Personalism of John Henry Newman* (Washington, DC: Catholic University of America Press, 2014), chap. 4, esp. 88–110.

17. Aidan Nichols, *The Word Has Been Abroad* (Washington, DC: Catholic University of America Press, 1998), xv.

18. Cessario, *Theology and Sanctity*, 67.

19. Robert Barron, *The Priority of Christ* (Grand Rapids, MI: Brazos, 2007), 32–33.

20. *Catechism of the Catholic Church*, no. 1777.

21. Paul VI, Dogmatic Constitution on the Church, *Lumen gentium* (November 21, 1964), no. 39.

22. Robert Sokolowski, *Eucharistic Presence* (Washinton, DC: Catholic University of America Press, 1993), 61.

23. "What is most mysterious is…precisely the infinite self-giving of God which is the fundamental characteristic of the divine Trinity and is enacted in history in the life, death, and resurrection of Jesus" (McIntosh, *Mystical Theology*, 44).

24. See Collins, *Diakonia Studies*: "*diakon*…Luke's choice of this word is not the result of casual usage. Nor is its presence in the narrative for the purpose of inculcating lessons about lowly service…. The only reason Luke uses the word is to contribute to the dignity of the occasion [ie. Christ attending to the tables]…*diakon* is recognizable to Luke's readers as marking the formal and religious nature of the occasion" (92–93). Collins's work continues to be controversial. His interpretation of the *diakon-* words that go beyond a narrow reference to service to the materially poor is convincing in light of Acts and other writings where deacons are seen proclaiming the word given to them even more than they are seen serving "the poor." However, in the Gospels, the word appears to include such direct service, which of course is not contradictory to proclamation but, in fact, is its embodiment. See Collins, *Diakonia Studies*, 245, where he notes the critique of his interpretation.

25. Joseph Cardinal Ratzinger, *Behold the Pierced One*, trans. Graham Harrison (San Francisco: Ignatius Press, 1986). (Author's emphasis.)

26. Marc Nicholas, *Jean Danielou's Doxological Humanism* (Eugene, OR: Pickwick, 2012), 78.

27. *Lumen gentium*, no. 41.

28. David Fagerberg, *On Liturgical Asceticism* (Washington, DC: Catholic University of America Press, 2013), 83.

29. Hans Urs von Balthasar, "Vocation," *Communio* 37, no. 1 (Spring 2010): 125.

30. Fagerberg, *On Liturgical Asceticism*, 159.

31. "Do not say to Him, 'I come to you because I am so well prepared, but I come to you because I need you so much" (Jean C. J. d'Elbee, *I Believe in Love* [Manchester: Sophia Institute, 2001], 244).

32. For examples, see Victoria S. Harrison, *The Apologetic Value of Human Holiness* (Dordrecht: Kluwer, 2000), 69; Gerald O'Collins, *The Spirituality of the Second Vatican Council* (Mahwah, NJ: Paulist Press, 2014), 5; and "From his fullness *we have all received*, grace in place of grace," (John 1:16, author's emphasis).

33. He does the same for the universal Church because the universal ecclesial mission is diaconal as well as being instantiated within particular clerical members.

34. See Crosby, *The Personalism of John Henry Newman*, 45.

35. *Lumen gentium*, no. 11. (Author's emphasis.)

36. Gisbert Greshake, *The Meaning of Christian Priesthood*, trans. Peadar MacSeumais (Westminster, MD: Christian Classics, 1989), 83-84.

37. United States Conference of Catholic Bishops, *National Directory for the Formation, Ministry, and Life of Permanent Deacons in the United States* (Washington, DC: United States Conference of Catholic Bishops, 2005), no. 113.

38. *Lumen gentium*, no. 41.

39. Han Urs von Balthasar, *Prayer* (San Francisco: Ignatius Press, 1986), 123-24.

PART IV
Diaconate and Action

8.

Identity and Mission

DOMINIC CERRATO

IDENTITY VERSUS MISSION

Since its implementation in 1968, the diaconate has struggled to find its voice within the larger Church. Its disappearance as a permanent order within the threefold hierarchy for over one thousand years has left the order theologically impoverished, leading to confusion as to the identity and mission of this sacred office. As observed by the Benedictine scholar Dom Augustinus Kerkvoorde just prior to the Second Vatican Council,

> There is, as far as we know, no independent theology of the diaconate. The number of authors and the works we cite should not delude us. None of them deals with the diaconate exclusively, say, to help deacons correctly understand and exercise their function in the Church. What we are left here with will only be individual fragments (*membra disjecta*) scattered throughout the various writing on orders in general, the priesthood, the sacraments or the Church.[1]

As later noted by the International Theological Commission, this *membra disjecta* can be clearly observed in both the conciliar and postconciliar documents on the diaconate. Of these, the commission wrote, "With reference to the pastoral priorities and in what concerns objective doctrinal difficulties, the Council texts show diversity of theological nuances which it is quite hard to harmonize."[2] In a similar manner, with regard to the 1983 revision of the Code of Canon Law, Fr. James Provost commented that there is "still no coherent treatment of the permanent deacons as a 'proper and permanent rank in the hierarchy' comparable to the treatment given presbyters and bishops in the code; rather they are treated as exceptions to the norms for presbyters."[3] As a result, both before and after the Second Vatican Council, theological consideration of holy orders focused almost exclusively on the episcopate and presbyterate.[4]

Nearly fifty years after the restoration of the permanent diaconate, there is still a sense among many contemporary theologians that the theology of the diaconate, and by extension its identity and mission, requires significant development.[5] This view is also shared by the United States' Catholic Bishops who, after their 1994-95 national survey of the diaconate concluded that "the challenge of the next decades will be to make these developments more theologically rich and thus to expand the deacons sense of ministry, evangelization and service continually, even beyond the parish."[6] In 2003, the International Theological Commission (ITC) published its research document, *From the Diakonia of Christ to the Diakonia of the Apostles*. The five-year study is a carefully nuanced theological exposition that traces the history of the diaconate from the time of Christ to the present. Despite the scope and complexity of the material and the clear and concise manner in which it is written, Fr. Richard Lennan observed,

> For all its good points, the document might well leave readers somewhat frustrated, as it tends to list the challenges rather than address them. Perhaps addressing them was not the Commission's brief, but while they remain unaddressed—to say nothing of unresolved—the place of the diaconate in the contemporary Church will continue to be problematic.[7]

Identity and Mission

Given the theological state of the question, it is reasonable to conclude that, to contribute more effectively to the mission of the Church, the diaconate must rediscover and deepen its own particular identity. This is the most fundamental of pursuits as it seeks to know what a thing is. Consequently, before one can consider how the diaconate contributes to the Church's mission in terms of ministry, it is first necessary to understand the diaconate. Simply put, there exists a primacy of identity over mission such that identity always precedes mission. So, for example, before we can understand the duties of a mother toward her children, it is first necessary that we understand motherhood itself. From this identity, we can deduce how she ought to act, thereby enabling her to more effectively fulfill her mission. In many respects, this understanding is simply an application of the Latin maxim *agere sequitur esse* (to act is to follow being). This means that what a thing is (*esse*) determines how it will act (*agere*).

Nevertheless, much of the early theological contributions to the diaconate after the Second Vatican Council tended to focus on what the deacon can do (mission) apart from who he is (identity). This resulted in a kind of dualism reducing the deacon to his functions with little or no regard for his unique identity as Christ the servant within the ministerial hierarchy. Consequently, the deacon did this liturgical thing or that ministerial practice because it was the most efficient way to meet this particular liturgical need or that particular ministerial requirement. As noble as this pragmatism may seem in meeting certain needs, alone it had the tendency of reducing the diaconate to its functionality and emptying the office of its sacred meaning and purpose. This "reduction to the pragmatic," and its ultimate conclusion, is exemplified in the work of the Augustinian theologian Fr. George H. Tavard, who wrote,

> Vatican II decided to restore a permanent diaconate, to be conferred on married as well as single men. This was clearly the start of an attempt at a minor restructuring of ministry. Yet this decision, I believe, was not carefully weighed. For the problem of ministry does not reside on aligning future practice on

ancient theory....In keeping with Parkinson's Law, superfluous work had to be created for the deacon. What a deacon is officially habilitated to perform can be adequately performed by a member of the laity. I would therefore suggest that the diaconate could be altogether abandoned both in practice and theory.[8]

Fr. Tavard casts the diaconate exclusively in terms of functionality such that anyone physically capable of performing these same functions accomplishes these same things. But does this really hold true? Consider the analogy offered by James Barnett when he observes,

> In a physical body, a particular organ, such as the eye, has been created to fulfill a certain function. It is true that the hands can fulfill some of the function of the eyes, but never so well as the eyes themselves. Although a layperson may assume a function of a clerical office, such as that of a deacon, it does make a significant difference that such a person has neither the authorization nor the grace of the office itself.[9]

In a similar way, does it really matter if a sick child is cared for by her mother or by a stranger? Both perform the same outward functions, but are they really doing the same thing? Does it really matter if the words of consecration are said over bread and wine by a priest or a layperson? Both perform the same outward function, but are they really doing the same thing? Is it rather that the mother and the stranger, as well as the priest and layperson, simply share an accidental likeness? In fact, they are doing substantially different things. The stranger and the layperson are merely simulating what the mother and priest, respectively, are really doing. Moreover, by adopting the flawed premise that "what a deacon is officially habilitated to perform can be adequately performed by a member of the laity," Tavard arrives at an equally flawed conclusion: "the diaconate could be altogether abandoned both in practice and theory." Furthermore, if this way of thinking were taken to its logical conclusion and applied to the priesthood, one may conclude that the priesthood could also be abandoned both in practice and theory.

Where Fr. Tavard takes this functionalism to one extreme, arguing against the diaconate, others take it to the other extreme. In extemporaneous remarks to members of *Carollo*, an Italian association of broadcasters, Pope Francis speaks of the sin of clericalism. Within this context, he recalls that while a cardinal in Argentina, he was often approached by priests who, in praising a layman, would ask, "Eminence, why do we not make him a deacon?" The Holy Father observes that because the layman fulfills certain functions in a praiseworthy manner in the Church, there was an immediate call by some clergy to clericalize him. In response to these kinds of requests, he would say, "Is he a good layman? He should continue so." In sharing this observation with the press, the Holy Father was not repudiating the diaconate. He was merely asserting that the conferral of this sacred office is not a matter of function. For him, such an approach amounts to clericalism as it fails to take into account that the diaconate is a vocation, not the sacramental elevation of a lay function.

Fr. Tavard's approach to the diaconate, along with the approach taken by some Argentinian priests, implies that there is a primacy of the things we do (mission) over the persons we are (identity). This approach fails to take into account the mystery of the person as a "human being"—not a "human doing"—and employs a reversal of sorts resulting in a reduction to the pragmatic. It allows mission, defined by pastoral necessities, to drive identity. Lost in this functionalization is the beauty and grandeur of sacred service as an incarnational mystery rooted in divine love in which the deacon becomes what he is, the person of Christ the servant.

The distinction between "pragmatism" and "mystery," though often overlooked, was not lost on many of the bishops of the Second Vatican Council as they sought to restore the diaconate. Of particular note, and counter to Fr. Tavard's pragmatism, is the contribution of the Belgian prelate Leon-Joseph Cardinal Suenens. Grounded in the mystery of the person, Cardinal Suenens resisted the common objection that the restoration is unnecessary since the ministry of the diaconate can be assumed by the laity. In a series of talks given in the United States in 1964, he refutes this notion, saying,

> No one seriously proposes taking a certain number of functions...and then bestowing them, as it were from above, in haphazard fashion and on any and all members of the faithful. What is proposed is to entrust such tasks solely to those who give objective and sufficient evidence that they have received the interior graces indispensable to the exercise of these functions. The reason for this, quite simply, is to insure that such exercise will possess the supernatural efficacy without which a true community cannot be created. For unless it possesses this, I repeat, the Church cannot be a supernatural society, cannot be the true Mystical Body of Christ, erected and built upon the ministries and graces which the Lord foreordained and bestowed upon His Church for this end.[10]

Because the diaconate is rooted in divine revelation, its identity is most fully expressed theologically. Consequently, any description of mission that flows from this identity will be expressed in the pastoral language of the Church. The relationship between identity and mission—and its analogies of *esse* and *agere*, of theological and pastoral, of faith and works—gives rise to a final observation whose pursuit exceeds the scope of this paper. When mission flows from identity, it reveals that identity in a concrete way. While a deacon is far more than his functions, when he engages in his mission through the exercise of his ministry with charity, fidelity, and joy, he reveals the identity of the diaconate to himself and to those he serves in ways that are tangible and palpable. In this sense, the relationship between identity and mission are both sacramental and incarnational.

Identity and Mission

KEY THEMES OF DIACONAL IDENTITY AND THEIR PASTORAL IMPLICATIONS

The previous chapters in this book reveal certain key themes, many reoccurring, that pertain to the sacramental identity of the diaconate. The contributors were given no instruction as to how narrow or broad they were to interpret "sacramental identity." As a result, they were free to venture into any area within the Latin Catholic theological tradition. Given their varied backgrounds, this produced works in scripture, systematics, and liturgy, allowing for a variety of contributions.

While there are many shared points of convergence, there is, at the same time, a fascinating diversity. Each writer circles the same mysterious reality—in this case, the sacramental identity of the deacon—each finding a particular access point based upon his theological background. The complementarity of this commonality and diversity has resulted in a rich and fascinating contribution. Here, we will summarize nine key themes as they relate to sacramental identity. Furthermore, many of these key themes have multiple points, some of which we may use as a "springboard" for reflection, which may not always reflect the original intent of the contributor.

Here, the term *pastoral implications* refers to the practical consequences flowing from the deacon's sacramental identity expressed in concrete acts through the exercise of his ministry. These acts not only reveal the deacon's identity to those he serves, but in and through him, Christ the servant. When exercised in charity and humility, diaconal ministry gives rise to an encounter with the divine and constitutes privileged moments both for the ones being served and the servant himself. To use more classical language, the pastoral implications are the activation of the deacon's potency. It is the *agere* that flows from his *esse*. It is the works that flow from his faith (Jas 2:14-26).

Theme One:
The Deacon Is a Complex Man

The deacon does not choose between serving the hierarchical, visible, earthly society, and the spiritual, invisible, heavenly enriched mystical body. He must serve them both. He is a man of the Church, and so serves one complex reality coalesced from a divine and human element, which means we will find him in the mystical and the mundane, as at home in the spiritual as he is in the street.

—Fagerberg

Dr. Fagerberg maintains that the deacon is a complex man as a result of his relationship with the Church, which is herself complex, and that his ministry must necessarily reflect this complexity. Consequently, as Dr. Fagerberg concludes, insofar as the Church accommodates the sacred and the secular, so too the deacon must likewise accommodate, or perhaps more accurately, incorporate both of these realities.

Such a complexity, which from a practical perspective is always a kind of balancing act, must begin internally. In other words, the deacon must inculcate a spirituality that embraces both the secular in terms of the practicalities of his marriage, family, and work; while at the same time, fostering the interior life. These are not to be seen as polar opposites from which the deacon must "close the gap" by reconciling the two. They have already been reconciled in Christ Jesus whose ministry of service the deacon shares. By progressing in the interior life, the deacon grows in intimacy with his Lord, enabling him to grasp and understand what has already been reconciled. Thus, just as Jesus' divinity does not swallow up his humanity, so too in diaconal ministry, the sacred must not swallow up the secular. Instead, the two, while distinct, must mutually influence one another so that the secular can inform the sacred of the situatedness and the sacred can inform the secular on how to act within this situatedness. The sacred and the secular represent two dimensions of the same reality finding their nexus in one person.

In terms of the pastoral implications of this complexity, the deacon must integrate the whole of his life. While in the secular dimension of his life, he is to reveal his diaconate implicitly. Simply put, he should express selfless service in a joyful way to his wife, children, and coworkers such that he bears witness to Christ the servant in an unspoken manner. Even those who do not know he is a deacon should say to themselves, "I don't know what he has, but whatever it is, I want it." Similarly, while in the sacred dimension of his life, he is to reveal his diaconate explicitly. In this regard, he should express selfless service in a joyful way in the exercise of the threefold *munera* proper to his office. His secular dimension enables him to identify with those he serves in the sacred because he also lives a secular life. This positions the deacon to meet those he serves where they are, enabling them, primarily through the deacon's own witness, to integrate this complexity in their own lives. Thus, the pastoral implication of this complexity identified by Fagerberg is an integrated life that leads to an integrated ministry.

Theme Two:
The Deacon Is a Man of Mystery

[The deacon] is a minister filled with the mystery he serves, and the mystery of Jesus is hypostatic and paschal.

—Fagerberg

Though it may seem apparent, we cannot give what we do not have. The deacon cannot reveal the mystery of God made known in the flesh unless he resolves to hold fast to the mystery of faith himself. How does he do this? Once again, we return to an element expressed in our last theme, namely the primacy of the interior life. It is here, in the depths of his being, that the deacon encounters Christ the servant to whom he was configured on the day of his ordination. This encounter, insofar as it reveals something while at the same time veils so much more, is mysterious. Here the deacon seeks not so much to understand in an intellectual sense, but to know in an interpersonal sense the one who calls him. Consequently, he seeks not to possess the mystery, but to be possessed by it.

The pastoral implications of the deacon as a man of mystery are not so much categorical in that the mystery can be expressed in particular acts. Rather, it is transcendental in that it is a quality that should penetrate and permeate every act. In this respect, he is a minister filled with the mystery he serves. This quality can be expressed in his demeanor, which can be described as the manner in which the deacon carries himself in the exercise of his ministry. Demeanor, in the diaconal sense, is the character revealed when the deacon serves selflessly and joyfully with a quiet reassurance of being permanently available. Just as there is an authentic priestly character devoid of paternalism, so too there is a diaconal character devoid of egoism.

Theme Three: The Deacon Is a Bilocating Man

The Deacon is a bilocating man....He unites the ministries of altar, word, and charity. He rides that river of liturgy from the altar to the street outside, which he serves by rubbing shoulders with the people of God in their secular life. He climbs the mount of Zion while drawing people from the streets and byways of the world to the source of eternal life, which he serves at the altar.

—Fagerberg

In this fascinating analogy, Fagerberg describes the deacon as one whom, by virtue of his calling, moves freely between two worlds, the secular and profane. Among the threefold hierarchy, this movement is unique to the diaconate. Prior to the restoration of the order in 1968, this task was taken up by missionary priests. They too moved from the sanctuary, through the nave, and out into the narthex. However, while they accomplished this task and accomplished it well, this ministry is not at its essence sacerdotal, but diaconal. These priests were ordained deacons prior to their ordination to the priesthood and that first ordination permanently and indelibly imprinted them with diaconal character. This is true even after their ordination to the priesthood, which is why liturgically the priest can assume diaconal functions in the absence of the deacon such as reading the Gospel and the dismissal. That said, this movement from the sanctuary, through the nave, and out into the narthex, while still accomplished by missionary priests, has been taken up more properly by deacons.

In his observation of the deacon as a bilocating man, Fagerberg makes a critical distinction between the transitional and permanent diaconate; a distinction that has pastoral implications within the clergy. Transitional deacons, while still in formation, almost never move from the sanctuary, through the nave, and out into the world. It's simply not part of their formation. This is not in any way to diminish the authenticity of the transitional diaconate in terms of their ontological configuration to Christ the servant. A deacon is a deacon regardless of whether he is transitional or permanent. It is, however, to suggest that transitional deacons rarely, if ever, exercise their diaconate in a bilocating manner. If this bilocation is central to the diaconate in terms of its sacramental identity and ministry, and I believe it is, it leaves the transitional diaconate somewhat impoverished. This may be one key reason why some bishops and priests fail to grasp the nature of the diaconate and its unique contribution to the mission of the Church.

Theme Four: Diaconal Identity Is More about Being than Doing

One becomes a deacon not by fulfilling a set of criteria that describe the diaconal office, but by being named as such by one who intends for the name to refer in the way past users had used the name.

—Bauerschmidt

Bauerschmidt argues against a Rahnerian approach to the diaconate that seeks to sacramentalize laity already doing diaconal-like service. Karl Rahner, SJ, believed that, since these "anonymous deacons" (a term used by Bauerschmidt) are already present and working in the Church and since sacramental transmission is possible, it is fitting and opportune to restore the order. Such a restoration would make explicit and thematic what is implicit and unthematic. Consequently, by ordaining these men deacons, the Church would boost awareness of an office already being exercised within the Church while at the same time increase its attraction, propagation, and appreciation.

Counter to Rahner's approach, Bauerschmidt considers the work of the American philosopher Saul Kripke. In his *Naming and Necessity*, Kripke argues against descriptive theories that understand proper names as synonymous with descriptions. In this approach, something is named because it is referenced to what it does and thereby represents a kind of compact descriptor. This is precisely what Rahner does when he observes that there are already "anonymous deacons." He names them by describing their function. Kripke argues instead that names are "ridged designators." Ridged designators, applied to a person, fix the reference of the person by designating, through a community of speakers, what he or she is called in all possible worlds. Kripke uses the example of Aristotle and observes that, if the philosopher died at age two never having contributed his thought to the world, he would still be Aristotle. Here, he is not named by what he does (descriptors), but rather what a community designates him to be called, in this case his parents. Applied to the diaconate, Bauerschmidt concludes that

> Kripke allows us to understand ordination to the diaconate as a bestowal of identity rather than making explicit of an identity what was already present implicitly, based on functions already exercised. This would seem to accord with the idea that diaconal ordination has more to do with identity or "being" rather than function or "doing."

Identity and Mission

Although earlier in this chapter, we discussed the primacy of identity over mission and the difficulties associated with a functional approach to the diaconate, Bauerschmidt, through his contrast of Rahner and Kripke, provides a solid philosophical underpinning to that discussion. A Rahnerian approach to the diaconate, with its primary emphasis on sacramentalizing functions already present, has led to a functionalization of the order with negative pastoral implications.

While this may seem a rather broad generalization, it is reasonable to note that, in his work with some bishops and pastors, the value of a deacon is often reduced to his ministerial function; the worth and worthiness of his office is often appreciated not in terms of who he is (*diakonos*), but what he can do (*diakonia*). This has the effect of "thingifying" the deacon and depersonalizing the relationship between him and his pastor or his bishop. Sadly, it is not unusual for a pastor and his deacon to have no other relationship outside of their ministry such that they are almost strangers working in the same vineyard. Similarly, deacons can see their value solely in what they do such that, when they are not doing "diaconal stuff," they can lose their diaconal identity.

Consequently, the deacon has value to some pastors only insofar as he can plug the "ministerial gaps" left by a lack of parochial vicars. Consequently, the unique contribution of his office and its place within the larger gift of Catholic ministry rises and falls in direct proportion to a ministerial need as determined by the pastor. If the pastor perceives that there is no particular need (*diakonia*), then there is no need for a deacon (*diakonos*). In this case, the diaconate is a *mere* means to an end and not an end unto itself. This is precisely why it is not at all unusual to hear a pastor say, "I don't really need a deacon (means) since between my ministry and the help of lay ministers, we've got the parish covered (ends)." This kind of response fails to see the unique contribution of both the diaconate in general and the deacon in particular.

Given his sacramental character, to suggest that a deacon is not needed in a parish is ultimately to suggest that Christ the servant is not needed since the deacon can bring Christ the servant to the parish in a way that neither the pastor nor laypersons can. By way of analogy, it would be like claiming that we don't really need priests to care for the parishioners as we have bishops and deacons who together can fulfill the same function. Just as this example is absurd on the face of it as applied to the priesthood since it fails to appreciate the unique contribution of the presbyterate, so too is it when applied analogously to the diaconate. This functionalization of ministry is quite pervasive and arguably represents the most significant factor in the nonacceptance of the diaconate by clergy, religious, and laity alike. At its core, clerical functionalism espouses a dualism that separates the material from the spiritual by elevating the pragmatic aspects (*agere*) of sacred service over and above the theological aspects (*esse*), thereby reducing its import.

Theme Five: The Deacon Brings about Greater Communion among the People of God

The diaconate can be structured so as to forge the bond of communion between the shepherd and his flock, and to foster the link between the Catholic faithful and those on the margins—even beyond the Church.

—McKnight

In his treatment on the sacramental identity of the diaconate, McKnight provides a simple yet profound insight on the nature of the order and its role in the Church. Drawing from conciliar and postconciliar magisterial documents, he makes a compelling case that deacons are called to be mediators, and as such they act as an intermediary between the higher grades of the hierarchy and the laity. They do so not to impede the dialogue between the bishop and the faithful but to facilitate it, rendering the dialogue more effective and pastoral ministry more penetrating.

Dialogue assumes a form of communication that is dialectic in nature. The deacon, insofar as he lives among the faithful, becomes, to use a patristic analogy, the eyes and ears of the bishop. In this regard, he brings to the bishop or his representative, the pastor, the needs and concerns of the faithful. Similarly, the deacon represents to the lay faithful the teaching, governing, and sanctifying ministry of the bishop in response to the needs and concerns of his flock. In this way, by serving as a mediator, he stands between the hierarchy and faithful not to obstruct the relationship, but to make it realize its full potential. In this role, the deacon provides a unique contribution to the mission of the Church while at the same time fostering greater communion among the people of God.

From a pastoral perspective, it is arguable that the dialectic necessary to foster communion is rarely exercised in the Church today. Certainly, the deacon is often tasked by his bishop or pastor to share new guidelines and/or instructions to the laity. Sometimes this requires parish hall meetings to get lay input. While these are not only rare, there is nothing particularly diaconal about the task since the same event can be equally facilitated by a layperson or priest. Moreover, these are singular events and thus do not constitute the kind of continual back-and-forth necessary for the dialectic to become a conversation. Consequently, that which should flow both ways, most of the time, flows only one way.

Generally speaking, it is interesting to observe that, once the laity comes to know deacons, they begin to identify with them. This is because, to borrow an analogy from Fagerberg, deacons are bilocating men. They live in both worlds and are at home in each. Thus, for example, the laity observes the deacon function at Mass and later may see him at a restaurant with his wife; they observe him at a funeral service and then, the next day, meet him at a little league game with his children. He is engrained in their world: the world of marriage and family; the world of jobs and bills; the world of broken pipes and uncut lawns. The laity experiences this mediation implicitly whenever they see the deacon, whether he is in clerics or in jeans. This identification with the deacon means that he can go places priests cannot, listen in a way priests cannot, and know in a way priests cannot. Certainly, priests go, listen, and know, but not quite the same way that deacons do. As a result of the deacon's "bilocation," he can bring to the bishop and to the pastor a qualitatively better understanding of the laity's needs and concerns.

In general, the difficulty with this dialectic lies in a lack of upward flow from the deacon to the pastor and the bishop. This is possibly because many pastors and bishops do not grasp the role of the deacon as mediator and therefore do not formally implement the structures necessary to allow this flow to take place. Without setting regular time aside to listen, the dialectic ceases. Thus, one way to overcome this dilemma is to help bishops and pastors better grasp the role of the deacon as mediator. From this fundamental understanding, structures can be established such as regular meetings and other forms of communication to facilitate the upward flow. The result of this upward flow is a restoration of the dialectic and with it, as McKnight observes, greater communion. It will also have the effect of rendering the bishop's ministry more effective inasmuch as it is directly responding to deeply felt needs within the community.

Theme Six:
Deacons Are Called to Be with Jesus

Perhaps what is most important today for those living out vocations of priesthood and diaconate is to recognize that what is spoken to the Twelve by Jesus at the time of their call applies equally to deacons; they are to be with Jesus (Mark 3:14) before they do anything.

—Carl

The primacy of identity, observed at the beginning of this chapter, and the essential role of the interior life to that identity, as noted by Fagerberg in theme one, come together in Carl's fine work on the *daikon-* word group. In his consideration of the Gospel and Acts, Carl draws the conclusion that *being with* the One who sends before *being sent* is essential to vocational identity. This *being with* is not to be understood as simply being physically close to another. Instead, it is being personally close to another or, to use a more common phrase, to be in a relationship with another. The Twelve did not casually accompany Jesus as though they were strangers traveling in the same caravan, engaging in light conversation. Being with means being in an interpersonal relationship in that they share a common life. It is this being with, this relationship, that Carl sees as "the core identity of anyone who bears the office whose name comes from the word group *diakon-*." If identity precedes mission, and if identity is shaped by a relationship (being with the other), then any serious consideration of identity and/or mission must be rooted in relationship, in being with Christ.

It is apparent to the casual observer that, much of what we call identity is shaped by our relationships. To relate, in this context, is to have a significant association with someone such that that particular someone profoundly impacts your life, giving rise to a deeper sense of who you are. Consequently, if one is identified as a son, it is because he is related to his father. If one is identified as a husband, it is because he is related to his wife. In a similar manner, if one is identified as a deacon, it is because of his relationship to Christ the servant and his Church.

Nowhere is this relationship more influential in establishing identity than when it is bound up in love. To combine an Augustinian notion with a personalist approach espoused by St. John Paul II, love is a gift of self that wills the happiness of the other for the sake of the other. In love, the lover offers not something, but someone, his very self. He does this freely and for the good of the other. In sharing himself in a selfless way, the lover renders himself vulnerable while at the same time extending himself to the beloved, inviting a relationship. This invitation is accepted when the beloved returns the lover's gift of self with her own gift of self, thereby forming a relationship. The impact of this relationship to the identity of each grows or diminishes to the extent of their willingness to grow or diminish in love.

For a mutual gift of self to take place, the two must spend time with one another. This is Carl's point regarding the apostles and later priests and deacons. He notes that before it is possible to fulfill their mission, the apostles must be with Jesus and come to know him by experiencing his love. This divine love, extended first through his incarnation and later manifested in his ministry, reaches its ultimate expression through his passion, death, and resurrection. In this gift of self, a gift of self by which all others are measured, Christ offers himself to his beloved—to the apostles and, through their apostolic witness, to the world. It is a love that resounds not only through the corridors of history, but in the hearts of all who hear the good news proclaimed. Those who respond to this gift of self with their own enter into a relationship that, as noted above, gives rise to a deeper identity, calling themselves Christian in the midst of the community. When this relationship grows in intimacy as in the case when a Christian man becomes a deacon, his identity and subsequent mission receive a new specificity and intensity.

The pastoral implications of this insight for the deacon are that he must not only have been with Christ, but he must continue to be with Christ as he continues his mission. Since Jesus is no longer with us as he was when he walked the earth, the place of encounter is most fully expressed through progress in the interior life and in the exercise of diaconal ministry that flows from this interior life.

Growth of the interior life, regardless of the vocation, can hardly be overestimated; for it is there we discover the depths of Christ's love for us and are, because of this love, capacitated to love others with greater sacrifice. It is within our interiority, through steadfast prayer, pious reading, regular retreats, and frequenting the sacraments, that we experience the living God. This effort, which is always a response to grace, is greatly aided by a spiritual director who gently and firmly guides the deacon toward greater intimacy with Christ the servant. It is Christ alone who can lead the deacon in the Spirit to the Father. In this sublime encounter, the deacon is transformed such that his identity as *diakonos* is affirmed and deepened and his mission clarified.

As essential as prayer, study, retreats, and sacraments are to growth in the interior life, alone they are insufficient. They must be accompanied by diaconal ministry. This is because the place of encounter extends beyond our "prayer closet" and into sacred service. Indeed, if we were to leave this world, figuratively speaking, through prayer and sacraments and view ministry as not equally essential, our attempt to find Christ would only result in passing him along the way. The Christ we meet in the sick, the poor, the undercatechized, and the marginalized is the incarnation of the same Christ we encountered in prayer and the sacraments. Just as the Word was made flesh and dwelled among us, so too the interior life must move from the Word (prayer and sacraments) to the flesh (ministry). They constitute two parts of the same whole and form a tension that must be maintained. Thus, without being with Christ, without encountering him through growth in the interior life, the deacon cannot hope to have an intimate relationship with Christ proper to his vocation. If this relationship is lukewarm, the deacon's identity will suffer and along with it his mission as Christ the servant.

Theme Seven:
Diaconal Service Is Cruciform

John invites us to look upon the cross in faith and see there the Son of God's free and total giving of himself for others' good, an act of self-emptying service for others.

—Wright

In his clear and cogent analysis, Wright considers the sacramental identity of the deacon as it relates to the cross of Jesus Christ expressed in both the Synoptics and John. Here, Wright examines how Christ's service, and by extension that of his disciples, receives its ultimate identity and essential quality from the crucifixion; that is, the gift of Christ's own life on Calvary. Similarly, Wright argues that the cruciform shape of Christ's service is foundational for those who share in his ministry. Of this he concludes, "Without understanding Christ as servant apart from the cross, we arguably cannot understand the sacramental ministry of the diaconate with its demonstration of cruciform love."

Wright fittingly observes that the ministry of the diaconate, precisely because it flows out of the ministry of Christ, is one that finds its truest expression within the context of a love that takes the shape of the cross. Earlier, we considered the role of love and described it as a gift of self that wills the happiness of the other for the sake of the other. Indeed, nowhere is this definition more perfect and exemplified than by Christ's death on the cross, the ultimate gift of self. Thus, where Carl deals with this love in terms of being with, Wright now describes the quality of that being with as sacrificial. Jesus summarized this quality when he said, "No one has greater love than this, to lay down one's life for one's friends" (John 15:13).

From a pastoral perspective, and combining the ideas of both Carl and Wright, diaconal ministry must be contextualized as acts of love, as gifts of self that will the happiness of the other for the sake of the other. The quality of these acts, the quality of diaconal ministry, is measured by the deacon's willingness to sacrifice. The greater the sacrifice, the greater the love, the result of which is the incarnation of Christ the servant in the here and now.

The deacon's selfless sacrifice, especially when it is exercised with charity, fidelity, and joy, enables him to enter into the world of those he serves. This is particularly true when he serves out of his own woundedness, sensitizing him to the woundedness of others. In this, he quietly pours himself out like a libation in a way that reveals Christ the servant who comes, in his very service, as a divine physician, healing those the deacon serves, while at the same time healing the deacon himself. This reciprocal quality means that, when he contextualizes his ministry in sacrificial love, the deacon not only brings Christ to those he serves, but he encounters that same Christ in those same people.

Thus, in responding to Wright's challenge of considering how diaconal ministry "bears a distinctive conformity to the cross of Jesus Christ," it is by the exercise of sacred service contextualized in sacrificial love. Such a life requires a death to self in the service of Christ and is, by this very fact, a participation in Christ's own service. As a result, it takes on a cruciform shape contributing, in its own particular way, to the mission of the Church.

Theme Eight: Jesus' Redemptive Work Is the Foundation for Diaconal Graces

The Son of Man's sacramental presence, as the sacrament of God, is the source of diaconal grace, identity, and mission. It is not quite true that there is no deacon in the Gospel of Mark; the deacon is the Deacon, Jesus Christ, Son of God.

—Miletic

Miletic asks two fundamental questions: Can the Gospel of Mark teach about diaconal identity, and if so, what relevance would it have for deacons today? In response to these questions, Miletic takes us on an intricate and well thought out journey through relevant portions of Mark's Gospel. He maintains that, while the *daikon-* word group does not appear in Mark as it does in the other Synoptics and John, it is nonetheless implicitly present in the ministry, death, and resurrection of Jesus Christ. "For the Son of Man also came not to be served, but to serve, and to give his life as a ransom for many" (Mark 10:45 WEB). It is precisely in this double focus of service and sacrifice that Mark bears witness to authentic servanthood. From this, Miletic concludes that the diaconal character of Jesus' redemptive work becomes the basis for contemplative reflection on Mark's diaconal graces.

There are a number of themes that can be drawn from Miletic's work among which we will focus on the redemptive characteristic of Christ's servitude. This characteristic is essential to diaconal identity inasmuch as it brings us to the end—to the *telos*—of that identity. The themes of complexity, mystery, bilocation, naming, greater communion, being with, and cruciform shape each describe aspects of diaconal identity; something of what a deacon is (*esse* = *diakonos*). Indeed, insofar as mission flows from identity, each one of these themes has corresponding missions that describe something of what a deacon does (*agere* = *diakonia*).

It is identity's connection with mission that leads us to redemption, for the mission of the deacon is inextricably bound to that of his Master's, and that mission is redemptive. By redemption, we do not simply mean salvation in some general and impersonal sense; rather redemption in the sense that the intimate union we seek with Christ on earth, through the forgiveness of our sins, is realized most fully in heaven. This redemption in the mission of a deacon is twofold. Where this mission, expressed in the exercise of his ministry, draws those he serves to Christ and is therefore redemptive for them, it equally has the capacity to draw the deacon closer to the one he serves and is, therefore, redemptive for him. Thus, the recognition of this final end means that both identity and mission are salvific. They have as their final end an intimate and eternal union with Christ.

This ultimate end has profound pastoral implications. These implications were taken up and expressed by Pope John Paul II in his 1979 Apostolic Exhortation, *Catechesi Tradendae*. Though directed to catechetics, its relevance is universal and can therefore be applied most fittingly to diaconal ministry, revealing its ultimate end. As a result, Pope John Paul's words can be reread using diaconal language in the following way:

> Diaconal ministry leads both the deacon and those he serves to experience the mystery of redemption in all its dimensions. It reveals Christ the Servant and the whole of God's eternal design reaching fulfillment in that Person. Accordingly, the definitive aim of diaconal ministry, through the exercise of sacred service, is to put people not only in touch but in communion, in intimacy, with Jesus Christ: only He can lead us to redemption; only He can lead us to the love of the Father in the Spirit and make us share in the life of the Holy Trinity.[11]

If identity leads to mission and that mission's ultimate goal is redemption in Christ Jesus, then it follows that identity is also bound to that same end. In this respect, the intimacy and communion experience through the exercise of diaconal ministry for both the deacon and those he serves is but a foretaste of heaven. It is to experience an intimacy that while transforming, is not completely satisfying here on earth. It longs for its complete satisfaction and that satisfaction can only be found in redemption, in the eternal embrace of Christ. Put another way, where diaconal identity finds its definitive character in such themes as complexity, mystery, bilocation, naming, greater communion, being with, and cruciform shape each of these, along with their corresponding missions must bring a little heaven to earth. They must draw the deacon and those he serves toward greater intimate communion with Christ through his Body, the Church. In this way, the pastoral implications of diaconal ministry is a participation in, and a longing for, a fuller intimate communion and, therefore, must necessarily shape the sacramental identity of the deacon and the mission to which he is called.

Theme Nine: The Deacon Is Permanently Available

The deacon is a man who is rendered permanently available to the servant mysteries of Christ through ordination; he is one opened to Christ by the "wound" of this sacramental character.

—Keating

Insightfully, Keating considers the identity and holiness of the deacon in relation to the deacon's openness to the servant mysteries. By virtue of the wounds received at ordination, the deacon is configured to Christ the servant. This configuration enables him to be "permanently available" in both disposition and mission not by reason of empathy, but because of the grace that flows from Christ's own passion, death, and resurrection. Cooperation with this grace sanctifies the deacon, enabling a kind of *kenosis* surrendering his ego, thereby making room to accommodate Christ and his mission. In this regard, the deacon sacramentally makes present the eager availability of Christ who came not to be served, but to serve.

The notion of permanent availability as it relates to sacramental character is intriguing both in its theological insights and pastoral implications. Keating rightly observes that this availability arises out of the deacons' particular participation in the pascal mystery of Christ. Here, most vividly on the cross and in the empty tomb, Jesus reveals the ultimate meaning of permanent availability. Even death, with its apparent finality, could not render final that which is, by its very nature, permanent. Permanent availability is a characteristic of divine love that is forever enduring and unconditionally lasting. By virtue of his ordination, the deacon shares in Christ's love and, because of this, is now rendered to offer this love to others (1 John 4:10). He is capable of being permanently available to those he serves because of the permanent availability of Christ the servant to him.

While permanent availability as a quality of divine love makes sense, what is not so clear is that this love arises out of a wounding sacramental character. We often think of "wounding" as antithetical to love because it inflicts injury and represents, in this respect, a form of evil. Although this is certainly true in many cases, it is not universal. Where some "woundings" are clearly malicious in that their intention is evil, others are beneficial in that they merely tolerate an evil so that a good may arise. The difference lies in the direct and indirect voluntary. For example, an angry person may, in a fit of rage, attack another with a knife to the chest. This is clearly malicious. However, in an attempt to relieve a threatening pathology, a surgeon will make a large incision in his patient's chest. In both cases, the victim and the patient are wounded; however, these wounds are different in their respective intentions. They are both "woundings" to be sure, but their moral quality radically differs. One is damaging and destructive, designed to inflict injury; the other is therapeutic and curative, designed to bring about healing.

Of course, the greatest example of therapeutic wounding is the crucifixion of Christ. Though his divine nature did not need healing and his human nature did not need to be cured, Jesus nonetheless took humanity's place. Innocent though he was, he took on the ultimate wounding so that we might be healed. In this suffering, he demonstrated the depths of his love. Similarly, when the deacon surrenders to the wounds of his ordination, he participates in this redemptive love that results in permanent availability.

Thus, the kind of wounding that comes from ordination is beneficial of a particular kind. It is intended to restore the deacon to spiritual health through an exercise of divine love that is permanently available. It is about relieving the threatening pathology of sin and death that requires a kind of cutting-out so that the deacon can empty himself of that which impedes intimate communion with Christ. When the deacon surrenders to this wounding—which is as much a process as an event—he experiences divine love in the form of Christ's own eager availability to share his life. This experience is nothing less than grace and inspires him to become permanently available to others in both his life and ministry.

The pastoral implications of permanent availability lie not so much in being physically present, but instead, represent a kind of constant disposition of lasting accessibility. This is to say that permanent availability is not about cultivating a hyperactive ministry. Rather, it is an interior attitude of openness that gives rise to an awareness of the presence of Christ in those whom the deacon serves. This requires an exercise of the virtue of prudence so as to discern when to be active and when to be contemplative. In this respect, permanent availability describes a qualitative characteristic of diaconal ministry that admits to a double focus: availability to Christ through a nurturing of the interior life and availability to others through ministry.

CONCLUSION

From our consideration of these key themes, we can say that the deacon is a mysteriously complex, bilocating man who finds his fundamental identity in who he is, not what he does. He is a mediator, who mediates between the bishop and the people of God, bringing forth greater communion within the Church. For this to take place, the deacon must progress in the interior life, he must be with Christ the servant from whom he receives his identity, an identity that is shaped by the cross.

Diaconate and Action

This cruciform shape enables him not only to lead others more effectively to intimate communion with Jesus Christ in the here and now through permanent availability, but also to draw them toward eternal communion in the kingdom to come. While it is beyond our scope to exhaust the richness of each chapter, hopefully this broad sampling provides the kind of springboard necessary for a theological reflection that, in turn, reveals some of the pastoral implications.

At the beginning of the chapter, we noted briefly that the relationship between identity and mission is both sacramental and incarnational. In conclusion, let us now return to this observation.

The mission of the diaconate, revealed in its pastoral ministry, is an outward visible sign that points beyond itself to an inward invisible reality and makes present that which it signifies, namely diaconal identity. Because of this, the many forms of diaconal ministry are, "efficacious signs of grace, instituted by Christ and entrusted to the Church, by which divine life is dispensed to us."[12] In this respect, diaconal ministry bears fruit in those they serve with the proper disposition. Once established, sacramentality does not stop there. Diaconal identity, in sacramental causality, is only instrumental. Christ himself is the Principle Cause. Thus, where mission is a "sacrament" of identity, identity is a sacrament of Christ. This is the sacrament proper and is realized in diaconal ordination. Here the deacon, himself, is an outward visible sign that points beyond itself and makes present that which he signifies, Christ the servant. In this regard, he is the efficacious sign of Christ's grace because he has been called by that same Christ to act as servant in his stead. It is precisely here that the diaconate takes on an incarnational quality. By cooperating with grace, the deacon gives flesh to the *Logos*. Through the exercise of his ministry, he enables Christ to touch once again with human hands, to speak once again with a human voice, to cry once again with human tears, and to shed once again with human blood. This the deacon does in a way proper and distinct to his office, thereby contributing in a unique way to the mission of the Church. Thus, without a clearer understanding of identity, mission loses its grounding and its pastoral expression is diminished.

NOTES

1. Dom Augustinus Kerkvoorde, "The Theology of the Diaconate," in *Foundations for the Renewal of the Diaconate*, trans. David Bourke, et al. (Washington, DC: United States Catholic Conference, 1993), 91–92.

2. International Theological Commission, *From the Diakonia of Christ to the Diakonia of the Apostles* (Chicago: Hillenbrand Books, 2003), 92.

3. James H. Provost, "Permanent Deacons in the 1983 Code," *Canon Law Society of America Proceedings* 46 (1984): 175.

4. William Ditewig, *The Emerging Diaconate* (Mahwah, NJ: Paulist Press, 2007), 13.

5. William Ditewig, "Charting a Theology of the Diaconate," in *Theology of the Diaconate: The State of the Question* (Mahwah, NJ: Paulist Press, 2004), 34.

6. United States Catholic Conference, *A National Study on the Permanent Diaconate of the Catholic Church in the United States*, no. 16.

7. Richard Lennan, Review of International Theological Commission, *From the Diakonia of Christ to the Diakonia of the Apostles* in *Compass* 39, no. 1 (Autumn 2005), http://compassreview.org/autumn05/8.html.

8. George H. Tavard, *A Theology of Ministry* (Wilmington, DE: Michael Glazier, 1981), 91. The reference to "Parkinson's Law" is the maxim originated by Cyril Northcote Parkinson as part of the first sentence of a humorous essay published in *The Economist* in 1955. Parkinson states that work expands so as to fill the time available for its completion.

9. James Monroe Barnett, *The Diaconate: A Full and Equal Order* (Valley Forge, PA: Trinity Press International, 1995), 132.

10. Leon-Joseph Suenens, *The Church in Dialogue* (Notre Dame, IN: Fides Publishers, 1965), 84.

11. *Catechesi Tradendae*, no. 5.

12. *Catechism of the Catholic Church*, §1131.

About the Contributors

Dcn. Frederick Christian Bauerschmidt, PhD, is an associate professor of theology and chair of the Department of Theology at Loyola University, Baltimore. He received his doctorate through the Graduate Program of Religion at Duke University. His writings include *Why the Mystics Matter Now* and the *Blackwell Companion to Catholicism* (ed.).

Rev. Scott M. Carl, SSL, a priest of the Archdiocese of St. Paul and Minneapolis, finished his Licentiate of Sacred Scripture in Rome in 2008 and is an assistant professor of Sacred Scripture at the St. Paul Seminary School of Divinity of the University of St. Thomas in St. Paul, Minnesota. He is founding director of the Monsignor Jerome D. Quinn Institute of Biblical Studies and has recently edited *Verbum Domini and the Complementarity of Exegesis and Theology* (Eerdmans, 2015).

Dcn. Dominic Cerrato, PhD, is executive director of Diaconal Ministries. Formerly, he served in full-time pastoral ministry specializing in adult formation. He was awarded his doctorate in theology from the Graduate Theological Foundation and has over thirty years of experience in catechetical and pastoral ministry on both the diocesan and parish levels. Beyond scholarly and popular articles, he has authored *In the Person of Christ the Servant*. He and his wife, Judith, have been married for thirty-four years with seven children and four grandchildren.

David W. Fagerberg, PhD, is professor in the Department of Theology at the University of Notre Dame. He holds a doctorate from Yale University. His work has explored how the Church's *lex credendi* (law of belief) is founded upon the Church's *lex* *orandi* (law of prayer). He has published articles in academic journals, theological handbooks, and popular magazines and is the author of *Theologia Prima*, *On Liturgical Asceticism*, and *Consecrating the World*.

Dcn. James Keating, PhD, is director of Theological Formation, Institute for Priestly Formation, Creighton University, Omaha, Nebraska. He serves as director of the Deacon Office for the Archdiocese of Omaha, Nebraska, and is former professor of Moral and Spiritual Theology in the School of Theology at the Pontifical College Josephinum, Columbus, Ohio. He is editor of the *Josephinum Diaconal Review* and the founding editor of the *Josephinum Journal of Theology*. He has published numerous articles and is the author of many books including *The Deacon Reader* (ed.), *A Deacon's Retreat*, and the *Heart of the Diaconate*.

Rev. W. Shawn McKnight, STD, is pastor of the Church of the Magdalen in Wichita, Kansas. Formally, he served as the executive director at the Secretariat of Clergy, Consecrated Life and Vocations for the United States Conference of Catholic Bishops. He was awarded his doctorate in Sacred Theology from the Pontifical Athenaeum of St. Anselm in Rome. Prior to his appointment at the USCCB, he taught graduate courses in liturgy and homiletics at the Pontifical College Josephinum where he also served as director of liturgy, dean of men, director of formation, and as the vice president for development.

Dcn. Stephen F. Miletic, PhD, is currently a professor of Scripture at Franciscan University of Steubenville, Ohio. He obtained his doctorate from Marquette University. He served as dean of the faculty of Franciscan University from 2000-2004. Before that he served as director of the National Office of Religious Education for the Canadian Conference of Catholic Bishops, as well as provost and academic dean of the former Notre Dame Institute in Alexandria, Virginia.

About the Contributors

William M. Wright IV, PhD, is an associate professor in the Department of Theology at Duquesne University. He received his doctorate from Emory University and is a specialist in New Testament studies. Much of his work centers on the Gospel of John, its reception history in early Christianity, and the theological interpretation of Scripture in Catholic tradition. He is the author of *Rhetoric and Theology: Figural Reading of John 9* and coauthor (with Francis Martin) of *The Gospel of John*.